HUMAN RIGHTS WAT

TURKEY

Diyarbakir
Siirt
Mardin
Urfa

Lake
Urmia

SYRIA

Dehok
Rawanduz
Great Zab
Qalat Diza
Mosul
Arbil
Little Zab
Suleimanieh

Kurdish
Autonomous
Region

Dayr
az Zawr
Kirkuk
Halabja
Tuz

Hamadan

Tikrit

Kermanshah

Tharthar

IRAN

Habbaniyah

BAGHDAD
Tigris

Bahr
al Milh
Al Hillah
Al Kut
Dezful

An Najaf
Al Amarah

IRAQ
Euphrates
Ahvaz

JORDAN

Hawr
al Hammar
Basra
Abadan

| 0 | 100 | 200 |
kilometers

SAUDI

Fao

ARABIA

KUWAIT
KUWAIT
Persian
Gulf

IRAQ

Soviet Union
Spain
Black Sea
Turkey

| 0 | 1000 | 2000 |
kilometers

Mediterranean Sea
Lebanon
Israel
Syria
Iraq
Iran
Afghan.

Atlantic

Algeria
Libya
Egypt
Jordan
Kuwait

Ocean
Saudi
Arabia

Mali
Niger
Chad
Sudan

© 1990 Michael S. Miller

HUMAN RIGHTS IN IRAQ

MIDDLE EAST WATCH

HUMAN
RIGHTS
WATCH
BOOKS

Yale University Press   New Haven and London

Human Rights in Iraq was first published in slightly different form by
Human Rights Watch, copyright © February 1990.

Set in Times Roman type by
G&S Typesetters, Austin, Texas.
Printed in the United States of America by
Vail-Ballou Press, Binghamton, New York.

Library of Congress Catalog Card No.: 90-12830

ISBN 0-300-04959-5

The paper in this book meets the guidelines for permanence and
durability of the Committee on Production Guidelines for Book
Longevity of the Council on Library Resources.

10 9 8 7 6 5 4 3 2 1

CONTENTS

PREFACE

Human Rights in Iraq was originally published as a Middle East Watch report in February 1990. Many developments since then have affected and will probably continue to affect Iraq's human rights record, and its relations with other countries in a position to influence the way it treats its citizens.

As this book goes to print, Iraq has just occupied the kingdom of Kuwait. While it is too early to assess its impact, the invasion clearly alters much of the economic and policy context for the discussion in chapters 7 and 9. One day after the attack, Washington froze Iraq's assets in the United States, cut off virtually all trade, and ended loan guarantees and credits; some of these steps were recommended in this report because of Iraq's terrible human rights record. The Kuwait crisis is also forcing the entire industrial world, including the Soviet Union, to reevaluate its ties to the government of Saddam Hussein. We hope that the Iraqi government's disregard for human rights will weigh heavily in that assessment.

Hussein's government has in recent weeks made gestures toward improving the rights of the Iraqi people. At the end of July, the government proposed a new constitution that would set up presidential elections for the first time in the country's history. The text of the document is not yet available in the West, but Iraq's government-controlled media report that it will allow more political and press freedom and replace the Revolutionary Command Council—now Hussein's chief legislative and policy arm—with another chamber. How much the new constitution might change actual political and legal conditions in Iraq, however, is difficult to assess. As this report documents, Hussein's regime has largely ignored the many broad civil rights guarantees in the last (interim) constitution.

There seems to have been one improvement: an easing of the severe travel restrictions criticized in this report. While virtually all foreign travel was forbidden to Iraqis during the war with Iran, some people are now able to leave the country for business or vacation.

This freedom of movement has apparently not been extended to the Kurds. Several times in spring 1990, the government invited Kurdish refugees to return to Iraq and promised them amnesty. According to Amnesty International and Kurdish émigrés in the United States, more than a thousand people did return—mostly from refugee camps in Turkey, where food and medical supplies were in ever shorter supply. These same sources say that the Hussein regime, contrary to its amnesty, executed and imprisoned several of the returning Kurds and sent hundreds to internment camps in the southern deserts, far from the traditional Kurdish areas.

Unfortunately, these reports cannot be confirmed. The government—which denies that there have been any executions and says the émigrés returned to their old villages or to nearby developments that have electricity and running water—has not allowed human rights workers or journalists access to Kurdish areas.

Other than the developments covered in this preface, the report stands as originally published. As far as we know, the Iraqi government continues to muzzle the press, stifle political opposition, arbitrarily arrest people and detain them indefinitely without charge or trial, and torture and summarily execute political prisoners. We hope that if Hussein is serious about improving his human rights record, he will help promulgate a constitution that truly guarantees freedoms and let concerned outsiders see for themselves how well he is doing.

Human Rights in Iraq was researched and written by David A. Korn, a consultant to Middle East Watch, one of the five Watch Committees of Human Rights Watch. Kenneth Roth, deputy director of Human Rights Watch, edited the report with help from Andrew Whitley, executive director of Middle East Watch, and Eric Goldstein, research director. Susan Kinsley, a Middle East Watch consultant, wrote the preface.

Middle East Watch wishes to express its appreciation to Roberta Cohen for providing significant materials on human rights and Kurdish issues, to Deborah Gordis for research assistance, and to Michael Hoffman for advice on international legal issues.

INTRODUCTION

This report on human rights in Iraq covers the two decades of rule by the Arab Baath Socialist Party, by far the longest rule of any party or group since Iraq became a state. During this time Iraq gained international prominence, in large part due to its enormous oil wealth, believed after Saudi Arabia to be the world's largest. Since coming to power in 1968, the Baath party and its leader, President Saddam Hussein, have used this wealth to enforce their rule through a system of control that Iraqis know as "terror and reward."[1] The pillars of this system are a generous welfare state, a powerful army, and an extraordinarily well-organized and effective police state.

Oil earnings have also made Iraq a coveted market for the industrialized nations. This substantial economic factor, reinforced by increasingly influential pro-Iraq lobbies, has provided an important incentive to the West to disregard brutal and widespread Iraqi abuses.

In recent years, the Iraqi government has shed the external image of extreme radicalism that it cultivated during the 1960s and 1970s. It has loosened its ties with the Soviet Union, moved to what is commonly called the moderate Arab camp, improved its relations with the West, and sought recognition as a responsible member of the world community. After the fall of the Shah, Iraq came to be seen by many in the West as a bulwark against the spread of Islamic fundamentalism from Iran to the other oil-rich countries of the Persian Gulf.

Regrettably, the Iraqi government's shift toward a more moderate foreign policy has not been accompanied by a less repressive domestic policy. For over a year—since the end of the Iran-Iraq War—Iraq's leaders have spoken of plans for "reform" and have professed a desire to see human rights protected.[2] But little has come of these statements. Iraq's citizens continue to be denied freedom of expression and association, and to be subjected to arbitrary arrest and imprisonment, deportation, torture, disappearance, and summary and political execution.

Iraq's Kurdish minority has suffered particularly severe repression in recent years. After using chemical weapons to crush a Kurdish insurgency in 1987 and 1988, the Iraqi government is now engaged in a forced relocation program of such proportions that it threatens Kurdish ethnic identity and cultural survival. The goal appears to be to cut off Iraqi Kurds from their brethren in neighboring countries and to ensure that an active Kurdish insurgency cannot revive.

Reporting on Iraq is no simple matter, the less so when the subject is human rights. The Iraqi government does not allow independent human rights monitors, domestic or foreign, to conduct investigations in Iraq.[3] In 1983, Amnesty International was allowed to send representatives to Iraq to "discuss matters of concern" with government officials, but it was not permitted to investigate abuses independently. Middle East Watch's request to visit Iraq in connection with the preparation of this report was received with much courtesy by Ambassador Abdul Amir al-Anbari when its representative called on him in Washington on June 27, 1989, but later inquiries at the Iraqi embassy were met with transparent excuses and, finally, silence. A further request made directly to the Iraqi Foreign Minister proved equally fruitless.

The severe punishment meted out to Iraqi citizens who speak out on human rights intimidates others from doing so.[4] Travel restrictions imposed in 1979 and tightened during the Iran-Iraq War remain in effect and bar all but a few from leaving the country and providing testimony abroad. And the collapse of the Kurdish rebellion has closed off an avenue of escape and a channel for transmitting information on human rights abuses. In this sense, at least, Iraq today is even more tightly sealed against foreign inquiry than it was during the war.

Iraqi émigrés who seek to expose Iraqi human rights abuses live in fear of violence at the hands of Iraq's overseas security operatives. Many émigrés hesitate to testify even anonymously about abuses that they have suffered or witnessed, for fear of discovery and retribution against themselves or their families.

The Western press has had no regular access to Iraq over the past twenty years. In the last few years journalists have been allowed to visit Iraq more frequently, but in almost all cases on tightly supervised, stage-managed tours. Iraq's press—government-owned, government-operated, and tightly controlled—is not a source of information on human rights violations. Even in this era of improved relations with Iraq, Western embassy personnel still find themselves cut off from all but perfunctory contact with ordinary Iraqi citizens and severely limited contact with Iraqi officials.[5] Diplomats who have tried to move beyond approved bounds have met with reprisal. For example, in September 1988, the Iraqi government expelled a senior officer of the U.S. embassy in Baghdad, evidently because he spent too much time in Kurdish areas asking about the government's use of chemical weapons against the Kurds.

Despite being prevented from visiting Iraq, Middle East Watch has been able to assemble a large body of information on human rights conditions there. This book, originally issued as a report, is based on scores of interviews conducted in the United States and Western Europe with Arab and Kurdish Iraqis, officials of governments and international organizations, scholars, journalists, human rights experts, and various visitors to Iraq. The Middle East Watch investigator also examined extensive written documentation on Iraqi rights practices, for despite the Iraqi government's persistent and determined efforts to stifle the flow of information about rights conditions inside its borders, such information can be found in works of scholarship, reports and articles by Western journalists and other visitors to Iraq, public testimony given by Iraqi exiles, United Nations documentation, studies by human rights organizations and, finally, but by no means the least revealing, official Iraqi government texts. Taken together these sources of information cast a broad beam of light on the human rights practices of the Iraqi regime. The secrecy in which the government of Iraq shrouds its actions made it impossible to obtain proof of some of the allegations made against it. Where verification could not be obtained, Middle East Watch consulted recognized experts and matched the testimony of witnesses against one another. Only when there was concurrence among experts and in the testimony of several reliable witnesses from a variety of backgrounds was a particular incident or practice credited; this lead to the excision of a substantial body of material—some of it plausible—for which supporting testimony from experts or witnesses could not be found. If we have erred in this report we believe it is on the side of caution. Although Middle East Watch would have preferred to interview Iraqi officials and obtain their responses to some of the allegations, the Iraqi government's refusal to permit us to visit made this impossible.

A NOTE ON TRANSLITERATION

The Kurds of Iraq use the Arabic alphabet to write their language. Transliteration of Arabic and Kurdish names to English or other languages that employ the Latin alphabet at times produces a bewildering variety of spellings. In the matter of personal names, one may, for example, encounter Hussein or Husayn; Nasser or Naser; Mohammed, Mohamed, or Muhammad. Place names, too, often lack a standard spelling, unless they refer to a state or a capital city—for example, Cairo or Baghdad. The three major Kurdish cities of Iraq may be found rendered into English under the names Suleimanieh or Sulaymaniyah; Arbil or Irbil; Dahok, Dehok, or Dhawk. Various attempts have been made to standardize the transliteration of names from the Arabic alphabet but none has succeeded in establishing its monoply. As there is no sure way to escape confusion in this matter, the spellings used herein have been chosen less for linguistic purity than for commonness of usage and ease of comprehension by the Western reader.

VITAL STATISTICS

Official Name: Republic of Iraq

Area: 434,934 square kilometers, shares borders with Iran, Turkey, Syria, Jordan, Saudi Arabia, and Kuwait.

Population: 16 million (1986 estimate).

Ethnic Groups: Arabs, 70–75 percent; Kurds, 20–25 percent; Persians, Luris, Turcomans, 5 percent.

Religous Groups: Muslims, 95 percent (55 percent Shia, 50 percent Sunni); Christians, Yazidis, Sabeans, 5 percent.

Official Languages: Arabic and Kurdish (Kurdish used officially only in the Kurdish Autonomous Region).

Government:

The Revolutionary Command Council is the highest executive and legislative body. Saddam Hussein presides over the council, which currently has nine members.

The president of the Republic and the Council of Ministers are appointed by the Revolutionary Command Council. Saddam Hussein is president of the Republic and prime minister.

The National Assembly, composed of 250 members, was established in 1980. Later elections were held in 1984 and 1989.

The Judicial System includes civil and religious courts, criminal courts, and special courts for political and security offenses.

Administrative subdivisions: 18 provinces. Kurdish Autonomous Region established in 1974.

Legal Political Parties: Arab Baath Socialist Party and two small government-approved Kurdish parties, the Kurdish Democratic Party (non-Barzani) and the Kurdish Republican Party.

Economy:

National Income: $40.5 billion (1985).

Per Capita Income: $2,605 (1985).

Foreign Debt: $60 to $80 billion (estimated).

Natural Resources: Oil (government claims proven reserves of 100 billion barrels), natural gas, phosphates, and sulphur.

Iraq is party to the following international human rights treaties:

The International Covenant on Civil and Political Rights; signed February 18, 1969, ratified January 25, 1971. Reservations: Does not recognize Israel, does not endorse the Optional Protocol (which provides for petition by individuals against governmental violations of human rights).

International Covenant on Economic, Social and Cultural Rights; signed February 18, 1969, ratified January 25, 1971. Reservations: same as above.

Convention on the Prevention and Punishment of the Crime of Genocide; Accession, January 20, 1959.

International Convention on the Elimination of All Forms of Racial Discrimination; signed February 18, 1969, ratified January 14, 1970. Reservations: Does not accept the compulsory jurisdiction of the International Court of Justice.

Iraq is not a party to the Convention Against Torture and other Cruel, Inhuman or Degrading Treatment or Punishment, but the government has declared that it is considering acceding to the Convention. The Iraqi government also has announced "voluntary compliance" with the provisions of the Declaration on the Protection of all Persons from Being Subjected to Torture or other Cruel, Inhuman or Degrading Treatment or Punishment, adopted by the United Nations General Assembly on December 10, 1984.

Iraq is a party to the following conventions on armed conflict:

The Geneva Protocol of 1925 banning the use in war of chemical weapons.

The four Geneva Conventions of 1949. (Iraq has not signed the two additional protocols of 1977.)

HUMAN RIGHTS IN IRAQ

1

BACKGROUND

POPULATION

Iraq's population, estimated at 16 million in 1986, is composed of three main groups: Shia Muslim Arabs, Sunni Muslim Arabs, and Kurds. Shia Muslim Arabs are indisputably the largest of the three. They live mainly in the southern and central parts of the country and, in the view of most writers on Iraq, comprise 50 to 55 percent of the population. Sunni Muslim Arabs make up an estimated 20 percent of Iraq's population; they are native to the central and north-central areas, and in the past have made up the majority of the population of Baghdad. The Kurds, who for the most part are also Sunni Muslims, are a people of Indo-European stock with their own language and customs. They have traditionally inhabited the northern highlands and mountain region, where they form the overwhelming majority of the population, but there is much dispute about their numbers. Kurdish writers have claimed that Kurds make up more than one-quarter of Iraq's total population.[1] Others put the number at between 15 and 20 percent.[2] Assyrian and Chaldean Christians, Persians, and Turcomans make up the small remainder of the population. Until 1948, Iraq had a Jewish population that numbered approximately 120,000; no more than a few hundred remain today.

HISTORY

The British pieced Iraq together after World War I from the three Ottoman Wilayets (provinces) of Basra, Baghdad, and Mosul. Predominantly Kurdish Mosul was added hastily at the end of the war so as to assure Iraqi access to the substantial oil wealth that was known to lie under its soil. In 1920, Britain had the League of Nations award it Iraq as a Mandate State. The British proceeded to give the new state a king, Faisal ibn Hussein, a prince of the Arabian peninsula Hashemite family and a British ally in the war against the Ottoman Turks. The British also established a parliament, a judiciary, a government bureaucracy, and an army.

The artificial creation that became Iraq proved exceedingly difficult to govern. During the nearly four centuries of Ottoman rule before World War I, Iraq's diverse religious, ethnic, and linguistic communities carried on largely separate existences. They had little experience in living or working together and few common bonds beyond a shared antipathy to British rule. Despite stirrings of pan-Arab nationalism, the Sunni minority found its place in the new state more easily than the others. Centuries of being favored by their Ottoman Sunni rulers, particularly in access to what limited facilities the empire offered for secondary and higher education, had made the Sunnis the intellectual, professional, business, and governmental elite. They immediately took over the top government posts.

The Shia majority was composed mainly of poor peasants, though it contained a small but prosperous landowner and merchant class. The Shia often resented Sunni Arab domination but showed no inclination to rebel in mass against it.

Not so Iraq's Kurds. The borders drawn by the British separated them from the Kurds of Turkey, Iran and Syria and left them in a condition of perpetual discontent, motivated by fear of being submerged in an Arab-dominated state, and of disappointment over broken promises of an independent state of their own. Kurdish tribes revolted in 1922 and again in the early 1930s after Iraq became independent. From 1943 to 1945 Kurdish rebels controlled a wide area of northern Iraq; throughout most of the 1960s they fought the central government; and from 1974 to 1975 and again from 1983 to 1988 there were major Kurdish uprisings, each time in search of independence or genuine autonomy. From the 1930s until the Kurdish defeat in the war of 1974–75, these revolts were led by a powerful tribal leader, Mulla Mustapha Barzani.[3]

INSTABILITY AND POLITICAL VIOLENCE

In June 1929, Britain's newly elected Labor government announced its intention to grant independence to Iraq. This promise was carried out in 1932 when Iraq was accepted into the League of Nations.

Independence, however, plunged the country into turmoil. Instability and widespread political violence became hallmarks of the new state. In the summer of 1933, Kurds and Iraqi army units massacred several hundred Assyrian Christians, a minority that had been identified with British rule. From 1934 to 1936, three cabinets were forced from office by the agitation of rival political factions. In 1936, the army intervened and Iraq gained the dubious distinction of being the first Arab state to experience a military coup. Another six military coups followed in quick succession through 1941, when a government sympathetic to Nazi Germany and Fascist Italy seized power. The British promptly stepped in to oust it.

From 1941 until 1958, Iraq experienced a period of relative stability under a repressive, pro-Western regime, the chief figures of which were royal regent Abd al-Illah and veteran politician Nuri Said. In 1956 Iraq joined Britain, Turkey, Iran, and Pakistan in the "northern tier" alliance, sponsored by the United States and known initially as the Baghdad Pact. The move was widely unpopular and, together with public resentment against Abd al-Illah and Nuri Said, sealed the doom of the Hashemite monarchy. On July 14, 1958, the monarchy was overthrown in a military coup led by Brigadier General Abd al-Karim Qassim and Colonel Abd al-Salaam Arif, and abetted by the clandestine Communist party and the then fledgling Baath organization. The royal family was cut down in the palace and Nuri Said was killed and his body dragged through the streets of Baghdad. A crowd stormed a hotel and killed several Western businessmen and supporters of the monarchy. A number of prominent personalities of the old regime were jailed and four were later executed.

With the overthrow of the monarchy, Iraq again entered a period of violence and instability. Qassim took power but in March 1959 faced an uprising by conservative Arab nationalist officers in Mosul. Hundreds were killed in suppressing the uprising. According to one writer:

> The Communists and the Peace Partisans massacred the nationalists and some of the well-to-do Mosul families, and looted their houses. . . . An informal court was established by some Communists, and at least seventeen people, including some with no connection with the revolt, were summarily executed. All kinds of animosities festering beneath the surface erupted. Christians killed Muslims, Kurds attacked Arabs, and the poor looted the rich. [The leaders of the revolt] were taken into custody by Qasim on 20 September and they and eleven other officers were executed.[4]

Qassim soon fell out with his Arab nationalist, Nasserist, and Baath supporters. After a Baath assassination attempt in October 1959, he became increasingly isolated, and in February 1963, was overthrown and killed. The Baath seized power in coalition with conservative Arab nationalists and Nasserists and immediately massacred thousands of Iraqi Communists for alleged responsibility for the atrocities in 1959 in Mosul and Kirkuk. In the words of historians Marion and Peter Sluglett: "It is impossible to establish exactly how many people were killed, but many thousands were arrested and sportsgrounds were turned into makeshift prisons to hold the flood of detainees. People were killed in the streets, tortured to death in prison or executed after mock 'trials.' " [5]

This first Baath regime lasted only until November 1963. It was overthrown by General Abd al-Salaam Arif, Qassim's collaborator. Arif outlawed the Baath party and pursued its members. He was killed in a helicopter crash in April 1966. His brother, Abd al-Rahman Arif, replaced him, survived a coup attempt in June 1966, and governed until July 1968, when he was deposed in a second coup led by the Baath.

Since 1968, Iraq has been ruled by the Arab Baath Socialist Party. From 1968 to 1979, General Ahmad Hassan al-Bakr was President of the Revolutionary Command Council (RCC) and of the state. Saddam Hussein, who became vice-president of the RCC in 1969, emerged as the regime's strongman during the 1970s and since 1979 has been president of the RCC and of the state. From 1970 to early 1974, the Baath party governed in theoretical coalition with the Barzani-led Kurdish Democratic Party, and from 1973 to 1978, with the Iraqi Communist Party, though without ever relinquishing its monopoly on power. Al-Bakr and Saddam Hussein consolidated their power ruthlessly after 1968 through a series of bloody purges, the creation of a pervasive party and police apparatus, and the systematic rooting out of dissent.

THE WAR BETWEEN IRAN AND IRAQ

The Iran-Iraq War, as it is commonly called, was one of the longest, most savage, and senseless armed conflicts of modern history. It began on September 23, 1980, when President Saddam Hussein, evidently expecting a quick and easy victory over the Islamic fundamentalist regime in Tehran that had seized power from the Shah the previous year, sent his troops across the border into Iran. For the next eight years, until a cease-fire, sponsored by the United Nations, came into effect on August 20, 1988, massive armies confronted each other in fighting on a scale never before seen in the Middle East, along a front that during the entire course of the war moved no more than a few dozen kilometers in either direction.

Iraq mobilized over a million men and Iran fielded a force of comparable size. The two sides fought with extraordinary cruelty and ferocity. Iran used human-wave tactics, and drafted and sent large numbers of children to the front lines.[6] Iraq repeatedly used poison gas, in violation of the Geneva Protocol of 1925 that outlawed chemical weapons on the battlefield. Each side bombed and rocketed the other's cities. Losses on both sides were enormous. Iraq never made known its total casualties. Official figures issued by Tehran a few months after the war's end put the number of Iranians killed or missing in action at 194,931, but almost all other sources give a much higher figure.[7] In September 1985, on the fifth anniversary of the war, veteran *New York Times* military correspondent Drew Middleton reported that estimates made in NATO capitals put Iranian dead at between 420,000 and 580,000 and Iraqi dead at 300,000;[8] another estimate published a day earlier put total casualties on both sides—dead and wounded—at 1.5 million.[9] More conservative estimates made at the war's end put the number of Iraqi dead at from 1 percent to 1.5 percent of the population, that is, between 160,000 and 240,000, with Iranian losses two or three times that figure.

The Iraqi government went to great lengths to disguise the extent of the slaughter. After 1983 it stopped issuing casualty figures. Vehicles bearing bodies of soldiers killed at the front were forbidden to enter some cities and towns during daylight hours. The government banned public mourning and ordered families to keep funerals short, and the war wounded were reportedly kept off the street.[10] To numb the pain of personal loss, the families of those killed on the front lines were recompensed with gifts of automobiles, houses, or money. Although a mild austerity program was put into effect after 1983, the government took care to keep the markets well stocked with meat, eggs, vegetables, and other imported foodstuffs as well as foreign manufactured goods. A U.S. journalist who visited Baghdad in 1987 was struck by how normal and peaceful the city seemed in the midst of wartime.[11]

At the same time, dissent was vigorously repressed. Members of Shia and Kurdish opposition groups, and persons suspected of membership in or sympathy with them, were jailed, tortured, and executed in large numbers. Deserters from the army were summarily shot, a policy that may have stemmed but did not stop the flow of desertions; some 40,000, mainly Shia Muslims, are believed to have fled the ranks of the Iraqi military during the course of the war, seeking refuge in the marshlands of southeastern Iraq or the slums of Baghdad and other major cities.[12] Even before the war broke out, and without even a semblance of due process, Iraq expelled across the Iranian border tens of thousands of Shias suspected of sympathy with Iran. Some were Iranian citizens but most appear to have been holders of Iraqi nationality.

The immediate cause of the war lay in the sharp deterioration of relations between Iran and Iraq following the return of Ayatollah Khomeini to Tehran in February 1979. Khomeini began allowing Kurdish guerrillas to operate across the border from bases inside Iran; in response, Iraq renewed support for Arab groups in the Iranian province of Khuzistan. Khomeini wanted to export the Iranian revolution, and Iraq, with its large Shia population, was the obvious first destination. In the fall of 1979, the Iranian radio began openly inciting Iraqi Shias to rebellion. Terrorist attacks on senior figures of the Iraqi regime in April 1980 were attributed to an outlawed, pro-Iranian Shia organization called the al-Dawa party, which received direct support from Tehran.

These mutual provocations aside, it appears that Iraq's leader, President Saddam Hussein, saw in the disorder that accompanied the Iranian revolution an opportunity to topple the militant Islamic government in Tehran and to establish Iraq as the dominant power in the Persian Gulf region. Hussein demanded that Iran withdraw from the islands of Abu Musa and Tunbs, which the Shah had seized in 1971 from what soon became the United Arab Emirates, and the Iraqi government called for the nullification of the 1975 agreement between Iraq and Iran which had given Iran the eastern half of the Shatt al-Arab waterway. Early in September 1980, skirmishes between Iraqi and Iranian forces escalated as Iraq bombed inside Iran and the Iranian army shelled Iraqi border towns. On September 17, Saddam Hussein officially abrogated the 1975 agreement, and six days later the Iraqi army began its advance into Iran.

Behind these Iraqi actions lay a confidence engendered by Saddam Hussein's assumption of absolute power in the summer of 1979 and by the steady build-up of Iraq's military might over the preceding decade. Believing that the war would be short and victory assured, Iraqi propagandists enthusiastically labeled it "Saddam's Qadissiya," after the seventh-century battle in which the Arabs defeated the Sassanian empire and brought Islam to Persia.

The assumption turned out to be tragically mistaken. The war bogged down into a bitter and protracted struggle. When it ended eight years later, it left Iraq with no territorial or political gains to speak of; with Basra, one of its major cities, and its southern-port infrastructure in ruins; with tens of thousands of families bereaved; with 70,000 of its men in Iranian prisoner-of-war camps; and with a foreign debt estimated at between 60 and 80 billion dollars. That Saddam Hussein and his Baath regime were able nonetheless to survive the war and the disaster that it brought upon the Iraqi people was, at least in part, proof of the effectiveness of the institutions of repression that they had fashioned.

2

THE INSTITUTIONS OF REPRESSION

The army was the mainstay of the repressive regimes that ruled Iraq from 1958, when the Hashemite monarchy was overthrown, until 1968, when the Baath party seized power for the second time. It played a major role in internal security and in stamping out dissent. It engineered three successful coups. And it intervened repeatedly in affairs of state.

Though a military coup returned the Baath to power in 1968, and though a Baath military officer, General Hassan al-Bakr, headed the regime for over a decade, the Baath party, under al-Bakr and Saddam Hussein, moved carefully and methodically to subordinate the army to its own authority. It did this through a series of purges and by saturating the army with the equivalent of political commissars—officers whose job it was to give indoctrination lectures and to check loyalty.[1] Senior command positions were filled by party members, and party cadres were assigned to units down to the battalion level.[2] Soldiers were prohibited, on penalty of death, from membership in or activity on behalf of any party other than the Baath.[3] Officers known or suspected to harbor sympathies for other parties—the Iraqi Communist Party, non-Baathist Arab nationalist parties, or Shia and Kurdish opposition movements—were in some cases retired or reassigned, in other cases jailed or executed. In a bizarre twist, the Iraqi army found itself transformed from instrument to object of repression.[4]

While harnessing the military, Baath party leaders also set about subduing the rest of Iraqi society, using many of the same methods. Today, observers of the Iraqi scene speak of the "Baathization" of Iraq as a process long completed. The party is the pillar supporting the regime and the institution most directly responsible for enforcing political and social conformity. But in the years since Saddam Hussein became head of state, the cult of the leader has assumed vast proportions and, in turn, has been employed as a test of loyalty

8

and a means of enforcing conformity. Both the rule of the party and the cult of the leader are enforced by various secret-police agencies, which instill the fear required to sustain the regime's authority.

THE BAATH PARTY

The Arab Baath (or Resurrection) Socialist Party was founded in the early 1940s by three French-educated Syrian intellectuals: Michel Aflaq, a Christian; Salah al-Din Bitar, a Sunni Muslim; and Zaki al-Arsuzi, an Alawite. It is a self-professed revolutionary party with a doctrine that combines in vague, romantic, and mystical language a virulent pan-Arab nationalism with a dedication to socialism. In its pristine form, Baath ideology calls for the creation of a single secular Arab state with equal participation by members of all religious and ethnic groups. "One Arab nation with an eternal message," is one of the party's early slogans. But despite its pretension to embrace the entire Arab world, the Baath party developed a serious following in only Syria and Iraq. Syria has been ruled by one faction or another of the Baath party since 1963. After the Baath seized power in Iraq in 1968, repeated efforts were made to implement the party's pan-Arab program by merging Syria and Iraq. All failed, supposedly owing to disagreement over points of ideology, but perhaps mainly because of personal rivalries and animosities between the leaders of the two states. Today Iraq and Syria, both still ruled by Baath parties, are at drawn daggers, and on opposite sides of almost every regional issue.

In recent years, all the main tenets of Iraqi Baathism have undergone substantial erosion. The idea that the Arab states could be merged into a single unit is now recognized to be impractical in any foreseeable future. The commitment to socialism is gradually giving way to an embrace of capitalism; although heavy industry is still under state management, the agricultural sector has largely reverted to private hands, and private management and capital are officially encouraged in services and light industry. And the Baath itself has become primarily a means to enforce political conformity and to mobilize the population for the benefit of the leadership.

In 1963, after it seized power for the first time in Iraq, the Baath party claimed a following of just under 16,000, only a few hundred of whom were full members.[5] The party's thin membership base was deemed to be one of the reasons for its failure to survive in power through the end of the year. After the second Baath coup in 1968, the party, under impetus from Saddam Hussein, then its second leading figure, undertook an ambitious recruitment drive, with the aim of putting down secure roots throughout the country. By 1980, through a combination of inducements, intimidation, and coercion, the Baath party had mushroomed into a mass organization with a following estimated at 1.5 million, over 10 percent of the Iraqi population at the time and perhaps 30 percent of the active adult population.[6] Relentless pressure to join the Baath party was put on army officers, government officials, professionals, teachers, and students. People who refused recruitment into the party were reportedly threatened, banned from teaching and entry into the university, and even arrested for short periods.[7]

Intensified pressure in 1978 and 1979 led a number of Iraqis to flee the country. One Iraqi émigré interviewed by Middle East Watch described what happened to him in these terms:

> I was only sixteen at the time and in high school but they kept coming around to me and insisting that I join the party. They tried to sign everybody up, and those who did join were then forced to become informers. I told them I wasn't interested in politics, I just wanted to concentrate on my studies, but they wouldn't take no for an answer. Finally we got scared and my mother and I left; my father followed the next year.

The party's various categories of members and followers are believed still today to number about 1.5 million. The core group of "active" or full members, however, has always been small; estimates of its size range from 25,000 to 50,000.[8]

In organization, structure, and method, the Baath party closely resembles a traditional Marxist-Leninist party. Hierarchy, discipline, and secrecy are its dominant characteristics. At the base is the individual cell, the neighborhood unit; followed in the hierarchy by the "division," which may cover a small city; the district "section"; and the provincial "branch," of which there are twenty-one (one for each of the eighteen provinces and three for Baghdad). At the top of the pyramid is the Regional Command, from which, in theory at least, the Regional Command Council, the highest executive and legislative body of the state, is elected.[9]

Like Marxist-Leninist parties, the Baath party is really a state within the state. It has its own training facilities, or "preparatory schools," where cadres and members study ideology, economy, and politics. The party maintains "bureaus" parallel to those of government departments which monitor and sometimes duplicate their work and assure conformity and loyalty.[10] These and other bureaus are charged with organizing and indoctrinating key groups, such as the military, laborers, farmers, and professionals. Along with the army, the teaching profession has been a major target for Baath party recruitment and monitoring because the party is anxious to assure the indoctrination of youth. In 1979, according to a variety of sources, all teachers were required to join the party, and those who refused or were deemed ineligible were fired.

The party also has its own secret police, the Mukhabarat, or General Intelligence Department, and even its own army, the People's Militia. The militia was evidently conceived as a counterpart to the regular army, to discourage the plotting of coups, and is almost as large. In 1980, on the eve of the war with Iran, the People's Militia reportedly numbered about 175,000.[11] During the war it expanded to some 750,000 and is believed to have stayed at about that level despite the cease-fire of August 1988.[12]

Through its pyramidal structure and vast bureaucracy, generally believed to include tens of thousands of cadres, the Baath party has penetrated all walks of life. Membership in the party is a prerequisite to political influence and an important asset for advancement in government, the military, or business. Apologists for the party claim that membership gives only a marginal advantage: "An incompetent Ba'thi is unlikely to be promoted, but all factors being equal a Ba'thi has a greater advantage than a non-Ba'thi," is the way it has been put.[13] This assertion is disputed by some Iraqis interviewed by Middle East Watch who say that nonparty members need to excel far beyond party members—in addition to being clear of suspicion of disloyalty—to be promoted ahead of party members. Stories abound of junior or incompetent persons being promoted over those more experienced solely on the basis of being members of the Baath party. Party membership is not required for entry into the university, but students who want to study abroad are told they must join.

The party's enormous membership and elaborate structure enable its leaders to mobilize and keep watch on all segments of the population. Civilian informers play a key role in surveillance. According to almost unanimous testimony, Iraq under the Baath party has become a nation of informers.[14] Party members are said to be required to inform on family, friends, and acquaintances, including other party members. Teachers reportedly ask pupils about their parents' views, with the result that parents feel obliged to disguise their thoughts in front of their children. *Index on Censorship* offered the following account of how the duty to inform can be enforced:

> One reliable report concerns a member of the ruling Baath party related to a former senior official, arrested in Baghdad in August [1987] after government informers reported that he had been present at a gathering where jokes were made about President Saddam Hussein. [The party member] was arrested for not informing the authorities, as were the male members of his family: three sons and a son-in-law. During interrogation they were subjected to torture. . . . [A]ll five were subsequently exe-cuted and the family's home was bulldozed.[15]

Almost every foreigner who visits Iraq has a story to tell about the oppres-sive atmosphere in a country where informing is a way of life. A U.S. student of Arab origin, interviewed by Middle East Watch, visited Iraq in the early 1980s and was first followed and then expelled after he went to the University of Baghdad to look for documents for a thesis, even though the research con-cerned a much earlier period of Iraqi history and a topic of no political sen-sitivity. A *New York Times* correspondent who visited Iraq in the spring of 1984 reported:

> The hotel lobbies are occupied day and night with idle men filling most available seats, playing with worry beads and keeping an eye on the guests, particularly when the guests meet what in most cases are their Iraqi business contacts. This enhances the claustrophobic feeling to which most foreign residents confess. . . . Whatever the degree of sur-veillance of aliens, it is far surpassed by the controls that the regime imposes on its own people, according to diplomats and other foreigners working here. "There is a feeling that at least three million Iraqis are watching the eleven million others," a European diplomat said.[16]

The Baath party assures its exclusive hold on power and the loyalty of its members through an extraordinary series of death-penalty laws. In a de-cree issued in July 1978, the Revolutionary Command Council made the death penalty mandatory for "retired military and police men or volunteers who are released from the service, or whose service has been terminated for any reason whatsoever after July 17, 1968, if their relation or work for, or in the interest of, any party or political group other than the Ba'th party, is proven."[17] Since military service is obligatory in Iraq, this law in effect bars the entire able-bodied male population from membership in or activity on behalf of any political party other than the Baath.

A series of death-penalty decrees promulgated between 1974 and 1978 assures lifetime fidelity by those who join the party. Since 1974, it has been a capital offense for a Baath party member to keep secret his previous party and political membership and links [18] or to have links with, or work for or in the interest of, any other party or political grouping.[19] Even by leaving the Baath party one cannot regain the freedom to join or work for another party, for in 1976 a law was promulgated that establishes the death penalty for former members, "if it can be proven that [they have] a connection with any other party or political grouping or [work] for it or in its interest." [20] Yet another decree, promulgated in 1978, calls for the death penalty for anyone who "recruits to any party or political grouping a person who has, or had, organizational relations with the Arab Baath Party." [21]

THE LEADER AND THE CULT OF PERSONALITY

The Baath party's formidable apparatus was shaped largely by one man, Saddam Hussein, and today it serves to put absolute power in his hands. The list of his titles alone tells much of the story. He is chairman of the Revolutionary Command Council, secretary of the Regional Command, deputy secretary general of the National Command, president of the Republic, prime minister, and commander in chief of the Armed Forces.

A Sunni Muslim, Saddam Hussein was born in the town of Takrit, northwest of Baghdad, in 1937. He joined the Baath party in his late teens, reportedly first as a hit man.[22] In that capacity he came to notoriety in 1959 as a member of the Baath party squad assigned to assassinate Qassim. Baath propaganda has glamorized his role in that particular incident to the point of legend: wounded in the attempt on Qassim's life, the young Saddam Hussein goes into hiding and, without anesthesia, coolly directs a fellow conspirator to dig a bullet out of his leg with a razor;[23] disdainful of the pain of his wound, he makes his way on foot and donkey-drawn cart to his home in Takrit, a journey of several days, in the course of which, through clever ruses of the "Thousand and One Nights" variety, he eludes capture, later to escape across the border into Syria.[24]

By the mid-1960s, Saddam Hussein was an assistant secretary general of the Baath party. According to officially sponsored legend, he masterminded the coup of 1968 that deposed President Abd al-Rahman Arif and returned the Baath to power. Whether or not this was the case, in 1969 he became vice-president of the Revolutionary Command Council, the second highest position in the state. For the next decade Saddam Hussein worked in tandem with President Ahmad Hassan al-Bakr, a distant relative and a native of the town of Takrit, while gradually drawing exclusive power into his own hands. Other relatives (who did not contest his primacy) were put in key positions in the security apparatus, the military, and the government. On July 16, 1979, al-Bakr, then sixty-four and said to have been ailing for several years, went on television to announce his retirement. Saddam Hussein took over.

The takeover may not have been the friendly affair it seemed. Some believe Hussein forced al-Bakr into retirement.[25] In any event, the transfer of power soon became the occasion for a massive purge. Shortly before Saddam Hussein assumed the presidency a large number of arrests took place. On July 28, 1979, the new president announced the discovery of a plot to overthrow the regime. Twenty-two senior officials, among them five members of the ruling Revolutionary Command Council, were sentenced to death and executed after what was described as trial by a special court.[26] Saddam Hussein and other remaining members of the leadership were said to have carried out the executions "in person."[27] These executions were publicly announced. A great many others are believed to have taken place unannounced. One writer puts the number of those executed secretly in the course of Saddam Hussein's takeover at some 500.[28]

Even some Western observers sometimes sympathetic to the regime thought it doubtful that there was really a plot to overthrow Hussein. Historian Phebe Marr put it this way: "Whether or not a fullblown plot existed, Husayn was taking no chances. He decided to inaugurate his presidency by making it clear, once again, that no genuine dissent would be tolerated, not even by his close associates."[29]

The cult of the leader existed in relatively mild form under al-Bakr, and he himself apparently did little to encourage it. Under Saddam Hussein, by the testimony of all who have visited or lived in Iraq in recent years, it has taken on vast proportions, surpassing anything seen elsewhere in the Arab world or, with the possible exception of North Korea, beyond it. Saddam Hussein does enjoy a degree of genuine popularity, in particular among those linked to the regime or who have benefited from it, and many Iraqis regard him as a kind of father figure, albeit a stern one. This notwithstanding, glorification of the Iraqi president has become one of the main enterprises of the country's press, radio, and television, and there is a thriving industry manufacturing posters, pictures, and other likenesses of him. President Hussein's picture appears on the front page of the daily papers regardless of whether there is a story to go with it, and calendars—each with a new picture of the president—are issued frequently throughout the year. Some two hundred songs are said to have been written in adulation of him. The evening television news begins with what Western diplomats in Baghdad call "the Saddam song," presented against a background of victorious soldiers and bursting fireworks by a smiling figure who chants:

> Oh Saddam, our victorious;
> Oh Saddam, our beloved;
> You carry the nation's dawn
> between your eyes. . . .
> Oh Saddam, everything is good
> with you. . . .
> Allah, Allah, we are happy;
> Saddam lights our days. . . .[30]

Families name children after him and young men imitate his walk and manner of speech. He has been panegyrized in film and in countless books in Arabic, and at least two extravagantly eulogistic biographies have been published in English.[31] In their early enthusiasm, Iraqi propagandists sought even to carry their campaign to the United States. An advertisement placed by the Iraqi government in *The New York Times* of July 17, 1980, on the first anniversary of Saddam Hussein's takeover, suggested that under his leadership Iraq was on the verge of repeating "her former glories" and compared the Iraqi president to Hammurabi and Asurbanipal of Mesopotamian antiquity and to the two great early Islamic rulers, the Abbasid caliphs al-Mansur and Harun al-Rashid.

The setbacks experienced by Iraq in its war against Iran, and Iranian demands for Saddam Hussein's ouster, brought an intensification of the cult of the leader. His birthday was declared a national holiday, and in 1982 members of the Iraqi national assembly wrote in their own blood a pledge of loyalty to him.[32] A U.S. visitor to Iraq in 1987 described the scene in these terms:

Larger than life paintings and cut out posters of Saddam Hussein are omnipresent in Iraqi cities and villages. The paintings, some of which are several stories high, depict Saddam in his role as Field Marshal, as a businessman, as a Bedouin Arab in characteristic headdress, as a Kurd, as a comforter of bereaved children, as a devotee in prayer at the holy shrines, as an air force ace, and as a cigar smoking politician. . . . He is venerated on screen and in print. Baghdad's new international airport is named after him; his face adorns calendars, clocks and watches.[33]

Iraqis say that a picture of Saddam Hussein on the living-room wall is a household necessity, if only to ward off suspicion that one is deficient in enthusiasm for the leader and his regime.[34] And as with so many other things in contemporary Iraq, the death penalty has been invoked to reinforce the personality cult. Public insult of the president or of the top institutions of state or party has been made punishable by life imprisonment or death. The decree, issued in 1986 and signed by Saddam Hussein himself, provides:

> Anyone insulting publicly in any way the President of the Republic, or his office, or the Revolutionary Command Council, or the Arab Baath Socialist Party, or the Government, is punishable by life imprisonment and the expropriation of all his property both movable and immovable. The punishment will be execution if the insult or attack is done in a blatant fashion, or is designed to provoke public opinion against the authorities.[35]

The second paragraph of this same decree stipulates a prison sentence of not more than seven years, or prison and a fine, for anyone found to be "publicly insulting in any way, the courts, armed forces or other public authorities and government bodies."

That these provisions are not just on the books but are enforced was suggested by Salaheddin Saeed, editor in chief of the Baghdad daily *Al-Iraq*, during a visit to London in 1987. Asked by a British reporter whether the Iraqi journalists' union would defend members who produced material deemed insulting to President Saddam Hussein, Saeed replied that his organization "does not represent criminals. . . . If you insult the President or the flag, you would be executed."[36]

Evidently, it is left to the courts to determine what constitutes an insult and at what point it becomes flagrant, for the decree in question offers no definition. Even an inadvertent slight can bring trouble. For example, British civil engineer Peter Worth told the London press that he was arrested, beaten, and tortured after he leaned against a wall at a construction project and caused a picture of Saddam Hussein to fall to the ground.[37] According to émigrés interviewed by Middle East Watch, even spilling one's coffee on the picture of Saddam Hussein that appears daily on the front page of the newspaper has been known to lead to arrest and interrogation.

This official personality cult is increasingly used as a means of political control. Observers of the current Iraqi scene have noted that taking part in this cult has become the new benchmark of loyalty, as important as joining the Baath party. For those Iraqis who choose not to become members of the Baath party, it in recent years has come to offer an alternative avenue for gaining access to the many rewards the regime has to offer.

THE SECRET POLICE

Observers of the Iraqi scene agree (at least in private discussion) that the secret police are omnipresent and operate openly with impunity, detaining citizens at will, making arrests without warrant, and routinely torturing and frequently murdering those in custody.[38] Published information on the Iraqi secret police is scarce, but a recent book sheds some light on the subject.[39] It lists three main agencies:

The Amn, or State Internal Security, said to have had close ties with the Soviet KGB in the early and mid-1970s, before the Iraqi regime's break with the Iraqi Communist party, but believed now to have been somewhat eclipsed.

The Mukhabarat, or General Intelligence Department, the Baath party's security arm, described as "the most powerful and feared agency . . . a meta-intelligence organization designed to watch over the other policing networks and control the activities of state and corporate institutions like the army, government departments and mass organizations." The Mukhabarat was headed by Barzan al-Takriti, half brother of Saddam Hussein, from 1978 to 1982 or 1983 (authorities differ on the date).[40]

The Istikhbarat, or military intelligence, which in keeping with the Baath party's policy of subordinating the military to its control, is said to operate only abroad. It performs traditional military intelligence-gathering functions but is also said to have been involved, along with the domestic secret-police agencies, in assassinations and other undercover operations on foreign soil.

Iraqi émigré sources told Middle East Watch that the Mukhabarat in recent years has been substantially reduced in size and authority, and that another organization, the Amn al-Khass, or Special Security, has taken over the role of senior and all-powerful secret-police arm. The Amn al-Khass is described as Saddam Hussein's personal secret police, run out of the president's office. Its rise to preeminence reflects the concentration of power in Saddam Hussein's hands. According to émigrés and an Arab diplomat interviewed by Middle East Watch, the Amn al-Khass is said to be headed by his son-in-law, Hussein Kamel Hassan, who is also minister of Military Industry and Military Industrialization.

Just how many people the various security agencies employ is one of the many unknowns of the murky world of Iraq's secret police. The Amn is believed to be part of the Ministry of Interior, which is also responsible for police functions and is said to be the largest governmental department in Iraq. In 1978 it was reported to have 151,301 employees, or nearly 1.5 percent of the estimated population of Iraq at the time. The Presidential Affairs Department, which presumably carries the Amn al-Khass on its payrolls, numbered 57,768 that same year.[41] Today both governmental sectors are believed to have grown still larger, both proportionately and in absolute terms.[42]

The Amn, the Amn al-Khass, and the Mukhabarat operate principally in Iraq itself, but because their activities are shrouded in secrecy, more is known about their operations abroad, where they cannot so easily escape public scrutiny. Even though foreign operations are undoubtedly only a small fraction of those at home, the list of assassinations carried out beyond Iraq's borders that are attributed to its secret-police agencies has grown quite long. Former Iraqi officials, as well as opponents and critics of the regime, have been killed in Arab capitals and in Europe.

In 1971, Hardan al-Takriti, a former member of the Revolutionary Command Council and a rival of Saddam Hussein, was assassinated in exile in Kuwait. In the late 1970s, several dissident Iraqis were murdered in Beirut and Cairo. London became the scene of two successful assassinations and one assassination attempt attributed to Iraqi agents or their surrogates in 1978. In January of that year Said Hamami, the Palestine Liberation Organization representative in the British capital, was murdered; although the killer escaped, the crime was attributed to the Abu Nidal group, a Palestinian terrorist organization based at that time (and until 1982) in Baghdad.[43]

In February 1978, Dr. Ayad Allawi, a senior Baath party official until his resignation in 1976, was attacked in bed in his home in the early morning hours by a man wielding an ax.[44] Dr. Allawi awoke in time to fight off the assailant, but in the struggle his leg was nearly severed and his wife suffered permanent injury; he himself required a year of hospital treatment to regain use of his leg.

In July 1978, former Iraqi prime minister Abdul Razzaq al-Nayef was shot in London on the steps of the Intercontinental Hotel. This time the members of the assassination team were caught; one was identified as an official of the Iraqi embassy in London, and another acknowledged being a senior Baath party member. They and the gunman reportedly confessed to the killing during police interrogation but later reneged and pleaded not guilty at trial.[45] The assassination moved the British government to expel several members of the Iraqi embassy and to issue a stern warning to Baghdad; U.K.–Iraqi relations remained tense for some time.

In 1979, gunmen operating out of the Iraqi embassy in Aden shot and killed several exiled members of the Iraqi Communist party. When the government of South Yemen took measures against the Iraqi embassy, Baghdad cut off aid and expelled South Yemeni students.[46]

Iraq is said to have been involved in the assassination attempt against Israeli Ambassador Shlomo Argov in London in June 1982, which triggered Israel's invasion of Lebanon. According to one report, the gunmen who shot Argov as he left a London hotel on the evening of June 3 were led by Nawaf Rosan, an Iraqi intelligence colonel who served as deputy to Palestinian terrorist leader Abu Nidal.[47]

Other assassinations are reported by Iraqi émigré groups to have been carried out or attempted by Iraqi services during the 1980s at a variety of locations in Europe, Asia and Africa, including:

Vienna, in July 1980, where an Iraqi embassy first secretary and attache were expelled for involvement in a bombing in which eight were injured;[48]

West Berlin, in September 1980, where a bomb was placed, but found and defused, at a meeting place for Kurdish rebel factions;

Dubai, in 1981, where Mohammad al-Salman, an Iraqi Shia and a member of the Islamic Opposition movement, was killed;

Sweden, in 1985, where Majid Abdul Karim, reportedly a former Iraqi intelligence officer who had defected, was killed;

Italy, in 1986, where Dr. Mohammad Habush, an Iraqi Shia and a member of the Islamic Opposition movement, was killed.

Pakistan, in March 1987, where Nima Mohammad Mahdi and Sami Mahdi Abid, Iraqi Shias and members of the Islamic Opposition, were killed.

Thailand, in May 1987, where Mohammad Zaki al-Siwaij, an Iraqi Shia clergyman, was wounded while leading prayer services.[49]

In January 1988, in an operation that attracted considerable international attention, Iraqi agents lured Iraqi Shia opposition figure Sayyed Mahdi al-Hakim, an outspoken critic of the Iraqi regime, from the relative safety of his London exile to an Islamic conference in Khartoum and three days after his arrival shot him down in the lobby of the Hilton Hotel. The get-away car used by the gunmen belonged to the Iraqi embassy. When the government of Sudan announced that Iraqi embassy personnel had taken part in the assassination, Iraq closed its embassy in Khartoum.[50]

Ismet Sheriff Vanly, an Iraqi Kurdish scholar and opposition spokesman who holds Swiss citizenship, has given a vivid description of an assassination attempt made against him in 1976 at his home in Lausanne. Vanly recounts, in a book published in 1980, that on October 3, 1976, Iraqi Ambassador Nabil al-Tikriti, a relative of Saddam Hussein, visited him, ostensibly for a discussion about the Kurdish position in Iraq. At the end of the visit, Ambassador al-Tikriti said he had brought Vanly fresh dates from Baghdad but had forgotten them in Geneva. He said he would have them delivered in a day or two. According to Vanly's account:

> On October 7, one of Nabil al-Tikriti's so-called diplomats called at my door. I invited him in and he put the packet of dates on the table in the living room, "with the compliments of Nabil al-Tikriti." I asked him if he would like coffee or an alcoholic drink. The killer, who knew the layout of my house, opted for coffee. I went to the kitchen to make some. I had just turned on the electric cooker when a shot rang out. The "diplomat" had fired at point blank range two 7.65 mm bullets which both smashed into my head, one behind the left ear, the other breaking my lower jaw. The medical report stated that the victim of this assassination attempt "escaped death only by an extraordinary fluke."[51]

Assassinations are only the most visible part of the foreign operations of the Iraqi secret police. Harassment is also common. Iraqi dissidents who have managed to flee have found themselves hounded from one country to the next. In an article published in 1986, an Iraqi writer who took the pseudonym of Raad Mushatat recounted harassment he encountered after he fled his native country in 1979. After escaping across the Syrian border, Mushatat traveled to Italy, where he and a group of other Iraqis started an Arabic magazine. According to Mushatat, "we suffered physical attacks from pro-government Iraqis and some of my friends had to go into hospital." Mushatat fled to the Algerian desert where, in 1984, he again felt compelled to move on.[52]

In the late 1970s, a rash of attacks on Iraqi dissident students in Britain by supposed Iraqi students under government sponsorship prompted the British National Union of Students to withdraw recognition from the Baath student organization, the National Union of Iraqi Students. Nonetheless, throughout the 1980s Iraqi students in Britain who had defected or who were known to be opponents of the Baath regime continued to be harassed by these "students." In December 1988, three supposed Iraqi students were jailed in Swansea for assaulting an Iraqi student at Cardiff University.[53]

Iraq's rapprochement with the West, its desire to gain respectability, and its need for Western credits to rebuild its economy following the war with Iran appear to have brought assassinations in Western capitals largely to a halt in the late 1980s.[54] Lesser acts of violence and intimidation continue, however. In October 1988, Britain, in recent years Iraq's most generous Western creditor, expelled three Iraqi diplomats on charges of "activities incompatible with their status" and asked a fourth not to return. The British press reported that the four were believed to have been spying on and seeking to intimidate the Iraqi opposition in Britain and that they had been found to be walking around London carrying firearms.[55]

3

THE CONSTITUTION, THE JUDICIARY, AND FUNDAMENTAL RIGHTS

As of early 1990, the Interim Constitution of 1970, as amended in 1973 and 1974, still was Iraq's basic legal document.[1] It establishes—or, more accurately, ratifies the earlier establishment of—a system of government wholly devoid of checks and balances, one in which many fundamental rights and freedoms are guaranteed in word but are routinely trampled in deed.

The constitution (Article 37) makes the Revolutionary Command Council—the small group of top Baath officials—"the supreme body in the state" and endows it with all the powers needed to run the state. The RCC is empowered unilaterally to promulgate laws and decrees, to mobilize the army, to approve the budget, to ratify treaties, to declare war, and to conclude peace. The constitution sidesteps the question of how the RCC came into being but provides that the RCC is to be self-selecting and self-perpetuating: it alone chooses and discharges its members, and new members must be picked "from among the Regional Command of the Arab Ba'th Socialist Party."[2] The RCC elects from among its own members not only its chairman and vice-chairman but also the president of the Republic. The RCC alone is empowered to amend the constitution.[3]

The constitution provides for the establishment of a National Assembly but makes clear that it will have only limited powers. Its main job is to "consider the draft laws proposed by the Revolutionary Command Council" and it is given exactly fifteen days from the time a draft law is submitted to do so.[4] The constitution says nothing about Assembly review of decrees—as opposed to laws—issued by the RCC.[5] The constitution authorizes the Assembly to return draft laws to the RCC if it disapproves of them, and if the RCC "insists on its opinion," the RCC and the Assembly jointly decide the issue.[6] Upon sponsorship of one-quarter of its members, the Assembly may propose laws on "affairs other than military matters and public security affairs."[7] The Assembly may "call the Ministers in order to make an enquiry or explanation," but only after obtaining the approval of the president of the Republic.[8] No provision is made for the Assembly to question members of the "supreme body," the RCC.

The National Assembly was not brought into being until 1980, a decade after the constitution was promulgated, and then only under strictly controlled elections. Either anticipating or responding to criticism that the Assembly was a powerless facade, the Iraqi government, in a report submitted in April 1986 to the Human Rights Committee established under the International Covenant on Civil and Political Rights, was at pains to let it be known that the Assembly had rejected nine of the thirty-two bills it considered in its session of November–December 1985.[9] The significance of this apparent show of independence is unclear, however, in light of the RCC's power to bypass the Assembly and rule by decree.

The constitution provides that "[t]he Judiciary is independent and no power shall be exercised over it except the law." Having stated this principle, however, the constitution fails to guarantee it. The judiciary is, in effect, left to fend for itself, at the mercy of an all-powerful executive that appoints and dismisses judges, controls the various police services, and rules unimpeded in all areas.

The judiciary in Iraq consists of religious, civil, criminal, and permanent and temporary special courts. There are also military courts, the competence of which is restricted to the armed forces. Serious criminal offenses are tried before the Higher Criminal Court, the judgments of which are automatically reviewed by the Court of Cassation, the nation's supreme court. Most political and security offenses, though, are believed to be tried not before the criminal courts but by permanent and temporary special courts. Foremost among these special courts is the Revolutionary Court in Baghdad, a permanent special court set up by Law no. 180 of 1968, amended by Laws no. 1, 85, and 120 of 1969. The Revolutionary Court is made up of three civilian or military judges, two of whom must be jurists. Sentences passed by the Revolutionary Court are final and not subject to any judicial review, although they may be appealed to the president of the Republic.[10] Temporary special courts appear to offer even fewer guarantees of due process because legal training evidently is not required of any of its judges. The temporary special courts that sentenced several dozen to death in 1977 and 1979 following anti-government riots by Shias in Karbala and Najaf reportedly consisted solely of members of the Revolutionary Command Council.[11] A temporary special court set up in 1986 to try cases of economic corruption sentenced people to death.[12] Special courts also issued large numbers of death sentences in the Kurdish areas throughout the 1980s, according to Kurdish émigrés interviewed by Middle East Watch. While the Higher Criminal Court and the Court of Cassation come under the jurisdiction of the Ministry of Justice, the special courts are run directly from of the president's office.

Iraq's constitution guarantees many fundamental rights, in some cases categorically, in others cases with reservations. Moreover, in theory at least, Iraqi citizens enjoy access to a still broader range of legal protections by virtue of their government's ratification of the International Covenant on Civil and Political Rights ("the Covenant"). Iraq claims that it has "undertaken to observe the letter and spirit of the provisions of the Covenant and has not imposed any restrictions on their application,"[13] and that the Covenant may be invoked in any court in the land.[14] The full Covenant remained theoretically in force even throughout the war with Iran. In its required periodic reports to the Human Rights Committee established under the Covenant, the Iraqi government prided itself on having refrained from suspending any part of the Covenant, as permitted by Article 4, "notwithstanding the exceptional circumstances that have arisen as a result of the Iranian aggression against Iraq."[15] In fact the Iraqi government routinely violates the most fundamental rights given in both its constitution and the Covenant.

THE RIGHT TO A FAIR AND PUBLIC TRIAL

Iraq's constitution does not specifically guarantee a fair and public trial. Article 20 states merely that "the accused is innocent until he is declared guilty by judicial procedure" and that "the right to defense is sacred in all processes of investigation and trial." In paragraph (c), however, Article 20 specifically provides for in camera trial and places no limit on this procedure.[16]

In theory at least, the International Covenant on Civil and Political Rights remedies the constitution's shortcomings in this area. The Covenant stipulates, in Article 14, that "everyone shall be entitled to a fair and public hearing by a competent, independent and impartial tribunal established by law." The same article also limits the use of in camera trial; it provides that the press and the public may be excluded from all or part of a trial only for "reasons of morals, public order or national security in a democratic society."

Ordinary criminal trials in regular Iraqi courts are said to be conducted publicly, with defense counsel present, and an opportunity to review evidence.[17] But the Revolutionary Court in Baghdad and the temporary special courts operate on quite different principles. By the nature of their creation and staffing, all are political courts and they appear to operate exclusively in camera.[18] The accused are frequently denied legal counsel, or counsel is allowed only at the last minute. There is no judicial review of convictions and sentences, in violation of Article 14(5) of the Covenant, which stipulates that "everyone convicted of a crime shall have the right to have his conviction and sentence reviewed by a higher tribunal." Iraqi spokesmen have argued that the absence of judicial review does not violate the Covenant because "any Iraqi citizen could appeal to the President of the Republic in order to request him to review a sentence passed by the Revolutionary Court."[19]

FREEDOM FROM COLLECTIVE AND RETROACTIVE PUNISHMENT

Article 21 of the Iraqi Constitution, which stipulates that "penalty is personal" and that "no penalty shall be imposed except on an act deemed by the law as an offense at the time of its commission," assures in theory full protection against both collective and retroactive punishment. But the Iraqi government has repeatedly violated both provisions. According to Iraqi Arab and Kurdish opposition sources interviewed by Middle East Watch, collective punishment is routinely practiced in Iraq. In Kurdish areas, people have been rounded up randomly and shot in reprisal for attacks on Iraqi troops or officials.[20] When persons wanted for political or security crimes could not be found, family members have frequently been arrested and in some instances tortured and murdered. Hussein Shami, a Shia clergyman from Najaf who was arrested in 1974, tortured, imprisoned until 1978, then hounded by the security police and threatened with renewed arrest until he fled the country in 1980, described an example of this practice:

I had gone into hiding in preparation for leaving Iraq. One week before I left, in February 1980, they put my wife in prison with one of our small children. They did this to pressure her to give information on me, and to put pressure on me to turn myself in. After I escaped she was kept in prison, and I have had no news of her since. My five brothers were also put in jail in February 1980 and I do not know what has happened to them either.[21]

Almost every Iraqi who has fled his native country to escape arrest has a story to tell of retribution against brothers, parents, or a spouse left behind. An Iraqi Kurd who came to the United States in 1984 told Middle East Watch that his mother and father were jailed for several months in 1988 after he took part in public activities in support of the Kurdish cause. An Iraqi student who defected while studying in the United States reported to Middle East Watch that his brother was jailed as a result of his action and remains in detention.

In addition to these many individual cases, there are several well-known instances of collective punishment in which penalties have been severe or large numbers of people have been involved. Among them are:

The execution by the Iraqi government, in May 1983, of six members of the family of Mohammed Baqr al-Hakim, an Iraqi Shia opposition leader in exile in Tehran, after he defied an Iraqi ultimatum that he cease making radio broadcasts. Another ten members of the al-Hakim family were put to death in 1985.[22]

The arrest and transfer to unspecified internment locations, in 1983, of some 8,000 male Kurds of the Barzani tribe living at the time with their families in a government resettlement village in Suleimanieh province.[23]

The arrest of some 300 Kurdish children and youths in Suleimanieh in northern Iraq in September and October 1985. Some of the children were relatives of Kurdish guerrilla fighters or Kurds who had deserted the Iraqi army; they were taken hostage in an attempt to force their parents or other relatives to give themselves up. Many were tortured and as many as 29 were reported to have been executed.[24]

In at least one case, the Iraqi government openly and publicly violated the prohibition of retroactive punishment set out in Article 21(b) of its constitution.[25] On March 31, 1980, the Revolutionary Command Council issued a resolution having the force of law that called for retroactive application of the death penalty to members or supporters of the Shia fundamentalist al-Dawa party. The text stipulated: "This resolution shall be applied to offenses committed before its issuance where no decision has been issued to refer thereof to the competent court." [26] When Amnesty International challenged this retroactive penalty during its visit to Baghdad in 1983, the Iraqi government argued that the resolution was justified on grounds that "al-Dawa is in fact a fifth column that strives to pave the way for the Iranian enemy to invade and occupy Iraq." [27]

THE RIGHT TO LIFE

Although the right to life is considered the most fundamental of human rights, the Iraqi Constitution does not explicitly recognize it. [28] The Iraqi government is, however, bound by the provisions of Article 6(1) of the International Covenant on Civil and Political Rights, which specifies, "Every human being has the inherent right to life. This right shall be protected by law. No one shall be arbitrarily deprived of his life." Article 6(2) then elaborates:

> In countries which have not abolished the death penalty, sentence of death may be imposed only for the most serious crimes in accordance with the law in force at the time of the commission of the crime and not contrary to the provisions of the present Covenant. . . . This penalty can only be carried out pursuant to a final judgement rendered by a competent court.

The Iraqi government has made a travesty of its undertakings under Article 6. Laws and decrees stipulating the death penalty have proliferated in Iraq in the two decades since the Baath party seized power. In its report of April 1986 to the Human Rights Committee under Article 40 of the Covenant, the Iraqi government listed twenty-four offenses that carry the death penalty, ten under the heading of offenses prejudicial to the external security of the state, ten for internal-security offenses, and four for "offenses constituting a danger to the public." [29]

Although most of these death-penalty laws concern offenses committed in time of war, some are cast in such broad and general terms that almost any act could be deemed to fall within their purview. For example, Article 164 of the Penal Code provides for the death penalty for "[a]ny person who, in time of war, attempts to jeopardize the military, political or economic situation of Iraq."

Similarly, Article 177 makes subject to the death penalty "the disclosure of a state secret" by a public servant "in time of war or in furtherance of the interests of a foreign state." In Iraq almost all information on government, economy, and society is considered a state secret. Foreign diplomats and journalists find it almost impossible to obtain even the most routine statistics from the Iraqi government, and foreign lenders wring their hands in anguish over the Iraqi Ministry of Finance's refusal to release data on the country's economic and financial situation.

Not all the death-penalty laws acknowledged in Iraq's report of 1986 to the Human Rights Committee concern acts of violence. Article 201 of the Penal Code specifies the death penalty for "[a]ny person who propagates Zionist or Masonic principles or who joins or advocates membership of Zionist or Masonic institutions."

Although the Iraqi government's report to the United Nations itself provided the above-noted extensive list of death-penalty crimes, it omitted many other laws and decrees that call for the death penalty. For example, the report made no mention of the laws that require the death penalty for Baath party members who keep secret their previous party affiliations, who keep ties with other parties, or who enter into a relationship with another party after leaving the Baath party. Nor was anything said about the laws that make it a capital offense to recruit members of the Baath party to other parties, or to carry on any activity within the ranks of the Iraqi army that is detrimental to the Baath party, or the RCC resolution that, on penalty of death, bars former military personnel from joining or working for any party other than the Baath party.[30] Likewise, no mention was made of laws that establish the death penalty for "economic crimes," or of the law that punishes adherence to the Bahai faith by fifteen-years' or life imprisonment, or by death in the case of Bahais who revert to their faith after having foresworn it.[31]

When Amnesty International's representatives visited Baghdad in January 1983, they expressed concern about the many laws that make capital offenses of political acts affecting the Baath party. Iraqi officials dismissed Amnesty's inquiry with the comment that these were "internal matters [having] to do with the Party's internal affairs and organization," the purpose of which was "the maintenance of the Party's ideological and organizational unity." Discussion of these issues, Iraqi officials added, "would be considered interference in matters which are not [Amnesty International's] business."[32]

Although in its report to the Human Rights Committee of April 1986 the Iraqi government professed to be "eager to protect the right to life," it continued to add to the lengthy list of offenses for which the death penalty is prescribed.[33] In January 1986, the RCC passed a resolution making "forgery in a passport issued by another state or any document issued by a competent authority in Iraq in order to obtain financial benefits resulting in damage to the national economy" a capital offense.[34] In April 1986, at the same time as it was submitting its report to the Human Rights Committee, the Iraqi government issued a decree making insult to the president of the Republic, his office, the Revolutionary Command Council, the Baath party, the National Assembly, or the government an offense punishable by life imprisonment, or by death if the insult is "flagrant."[35]

The majority of Iraq's death-penalty laws were promulgated after 1976, the year the International Covenant on Civil and Political Rights entered into effect. In decreeing the death penalty for several dozen offenses, frequently in language that is exceedingly broad and vague, and for a variety of wholly nonviolent political offenses, the Iraqi government violates Article 6(2) of the Covenant, which stipulates that the "sentence of death may be imposed only for the most serious crimes."

FREEDOM OF EXPRESSION

The right to free speech, opinion, and publication is severely circumscribed in Iraq. On the face of it, Iraq's constitution guarantees freedom of expression, albeit with important caveats, as a close reading of Article 26 reveals:

> The Constitution shall guarantee freedom of opinion, publication, meeting, demonstration, forming of political parties, unions and societies in accordance with the aims of the Constitution and within the limits of the law. The State shall endeavour to provide the means required for exercising these freedoms, which run in line with the nationalist and progressive line of the Revolution.

Requiring that the exercise of freedom of expression be "in line with the nationalist and progressive line of the Revolution" introduces restrictions that go well beyond those allowed under the International Covenant on Civil and Political Rights. Article 19(2) and (3) of the Covenant declares:

> Everyone shall have the right to freedom of expression; this right shall include freedom to seek, receive and impart information and ideas of all kinds, regardless of frontiers, either orally, in writing or in print, in the

form of art, or through any other media of his choice . . . subject to
certain restrictions, but these shall be such only as are provided by law
and are necessary, (a) for respect of the rights or reputation of others,
(b) for the protection of national security or of public order (*"ordre
public"*), the protection of public health or morals or the protection of
the rights and freedoms of others.

Iraq's newspapers, periodicals, radio and television stations, and single
news agency are all government enterprises, staffed solely by government
employees and subject to rigid political and ideological control. After the
Baath party seized power in 1968, it set itself the goal of bringing the media
under its control and making the media an instrument for propagating Baath
ideology. In a report issued in 1974, the party acknowledged that these objectives had not yet been reached. There were still too many "reactionary
elements" lurking in the media and too few "competent and revolutionary
executives."[36] In the ensuing years, these shortcomings were rectified. Membership in the Baath party youth organization was made a condition for entry
into the journalism school. In 1978 Communist party publications were shut
down and many of their staff members were arrested, tortured, and executed;[37] and journals published by Kurdish parties that were in theoretical
coalition with the Baath but were exhibiting unappreciated independence were
brought under control. In 1980, the General Federation of Academicians and
Writers was established, and all journalists, writers, and artists were required
to join; simultaneously, all existing cultural and literary organizations were
abolished.[38] All artistic production, even music, was brought under state control and strictly censored. Iraq became a place where, in the words of an Iraqi
writer who escaped in 1979:

> If you do show signs of talent in the field of writing or art, the regime
> soon recruits you into its service by offering all sorts of material incen-
> tives, housing, money, etc., in return for which you are taught intelli-
> gence work and the psychology of using art for propaganda. In other
> words, you become a state artist or an artistic consultant for the Ministry
> of Information.[39]

"For those who conform," one observer of the Iraqi scene wrote in 1981,
"there are excellent rewards. . . . For the first time in the country's history,
poets can be found among the wealthy few." The price of conforming is "to

write verse for official occasions and festivities, praising the ruling Baath party and its leaders . . . singing the praises of Saddam Hussein." [40] Failure to conform has brought imprisonment and torture, frequently ending in death, for hundreds of Iraqi writers and intellectuals. [41] In December 1986, the Beirut newspaper *As Safir* published a petition signed by Arab intellectuals stating that in Iraq "more than 500 creative writers and thinkers have been subject to questioning and torture in order to extort avowals or to oblige them to modify their opinions." [42]

Despite expectations that the government might relax its grip once the war with Iran ended, all means of communication remain strictly controlled in today's Iraq. Western publications are barred and Western films and television programs are carefully censored. During the 1970s, journalists entering Iraq found their typewriters confiscated at the airport. That practice has ceased, but visitors who bring in typewriters still find that the Iraqi police record the serial numbers in their passports. The Iraqi government's attempts to control Western reporters invited in to cover the early weeks of the war with Iran produced bitter complaints and clashes between the journalists and Ministry of Information officials. In an article describing correspondents' frustrations, *New York Times* reporter John Kifner recounted wryly: "Today, an English journalist who wanted to buy a typewriter here found himself applying for a permit in the office of one of the nation's ranking intelligence officials, where the chairs had manacles attached to them. He decided to keep writing his copy in longhand." [43]

Western journalists who have visited Iraq more recently have continued to encounter the most blatant interference by authorities. Reporters who were invited by the government in 1988 to check on allegations of Iraqi army use of chemical weapons against the Kurds were not allowed to speak freely with Kurdish villagers; television crews were required to turn their videotapes over to Iraqi authorities and a *New York Times* dispatch was first censored and then barred from transmission. [44] A U.S. journalist who spent several months in Baghdad during the summer of 1989 was obliged to stay in a room at the luxury Baghdad Al-Rashid hotel that had video cameras in both the room and bathroom. When she filed a story by telex, she later found it had been entirely rewritten by the Iraqi censor. [45]

Through its broad network of informers and secret police, the regime has succeeded in denying Iraqi citizens even the right to free expression in the home and among friends. [46] Free public discussion of political issues has been effectively banned since the Baath seized power in 1968. The decree issued in April 1986 authorizing life imprisonment or death for "insult" to the president of the Republic or any of the top institutions of state makes expressed dissent suicidal.[47]

Evidently in recognition of these restrictions, the Iraqi government sought to sidestep the issue of freedom of expression in its report to the U.N. Human Rights Committee of April 1986. Instead, it stressed the importance of using the mass media to "strengthen peace and international understanding" and to counter racism, apartheid and incitement to war. And it expressed support for the establishment of the proposed "new international information order" so as to "rectify the defects in the present system."

The report also claimed that the press and television in Iraq provide citizens the opportunity to "express their views and to criticize the erroneous application of laws and regulations," citing a television program in which citizens submit "criticism and questions in person to the officials concerned."[48] Iraqi citizens have in fact been urged to complain about government excesses, but so far only lower-level government officials have been criticized in the press.[49]

FREEDOM OF MOVEMENT

Article 24 of Iraq's constitution guarantees freedom of movement, specifying that "[n]o citizen shall be prevented from travel outside the country or from returning thereto." Article 12 of the International Covenant on Civil and Political Rights also stipulates that "[e]veryone shall be free to leave any country, including his own."

While the right to emigrate has never been respected by the Baath regime, through 1978 it was relatively easy to obtain permission to travel abroad to visit relatives, to conduct business, or to receive medical treatment. Since 1981, all but a favored few Iraqi citizens live under a de facto ban not only on emigration but also on travel outside their country. Exceptions have been granted only for a limited number of officials traveling abroad on government missions or officially authorized private business, graduate students whose study abroad is officially authorized, persons officially authorized to go abroad for medical treatment not available in Iraq, and Muslims for pilgrimage to Mecca. Even those students authorized to study abroad—always on government scholarship—are required to have a parent or other person guarantee their return; should the student fail to come back, the guarantor is required to reimburse the Iraqi government for the cost of all education the student received in Iraq and abroad.

The only persons known to have been authorized to emigrate in recent years—after paying substantial exit fees—are a small number of Iraqi Assyrian women for whom marriages were arranged with American men of Assyrian origin. American women married to Iraqis residing in Iraq have found themselves, and their children, deprived of the right to leave Iraq. Iraqi law requires that an alien spouse of an Iraqi citizen who has lived in Iraq for five years (one year in the case of spouses of government employees) must take Iraqi citizenship. Since Iraq recognizes a right of dual citizenship only for Arabs, American women who have been obliged to take Iraqi citizenship because of their marriages, and their children born of marriages to Iraqi men, have been barred from leaving the country on their U.S. passports.[50]

The need to save foreign currency during a wartime emergency was the reason advanced by the Iraqi government for its ban on foreign travel and emigration. Yet the ban was enforced even when the prospective traveler or emigrant proposed to take no currency or valuables out of the country. In 1985 an American Jewish organization petitioned through the Iraqi ambassador in Washington for some 120 aged members of Baghdad's Jewish community to be allowed to leave Iraq, entirely at the expense of the organization. The petition was denied on the ground that these persons—all too old to contribute in any way to Iraq's war effort—had to be subject to the same rules as other Iraqis.

During the war with Iran, the Iraqi government might have avoided violating the Covenant's provisions on freedom of movement by recourse to Article 4, which allows parties to derogate from their obligations in time of public emergency. Iraq chose not to do this and, as noted above, in its April 1986 report to the Human Rights Committee declared pointedly that it had not suspended application of any of the articles of the Covenant.

More than a year after the cease-fire in the Iran-Iraq War on August 20, 1988, the Iraqi government continues to flout both its constitution and the Covenant by barring its citizens, and those of other non-Arab countries who also hold Iraqi citizenship, from traveling abroad other than in exceptional circumstances. All but a privileged few Iraqi citizens find themselves trapped inside their country's borders.

In principle, Iraq places no restrictions on the return of its citizens, but in practice the right of return is circumscribed, though not so severely as the right to leave. The Iraqi government refuses to take back the tens of thousands—the Iranian government puts their number at 200,000—whom it arbitrarily stripped of citizenship and property and expelled to Iran after 1980.[51] Iraq has, however, sought to induce émigrés who are qualified professionals to return, by offering them a variety of incentives. Amnesties have frequently been offered for Iraqi citizens who fled to other Arab countries or to Europe and the United States because of their opposition to the regime or for Kurds who took refuge in Turkey or Iran. These pledges, however, have been frequently violated. Some of those who have returned have reportedly disappeared;[52] others have been denied the right to travel outside Iraq despite having been assured of such right before their return. For this reason, and because the Iraqi government has continued to deny fundamental human rights to those within its borders, large numbers of Iraqi émigrés have chosen to remain abroad.

FREEDOM OF RELIGION

Freedom of religion is guaranteed both by Article 26 of Iraq's constitution and by Article 18 of the International Covenant on Civil and Political Rights. It is the only one of the fundamental rights that the Iraqi government respects even in part. Islam is officially recognized as the state religion and its practice is freely allowed. The government pays the salaries of the Muslim clergy. While it does not appear to intervene in religious matters, it does closely monitor sermons for political content—particularly those delivered in Shia mosques—and it has ruthlessly repressed clergymen suspected of political disloyalty.[53] From time to time, Shia opposition figures said in interviews with Middle East Watch, the government has closed Shia mosques considered to be centers of political dissent.

The regime has, however, spent heavily to show its support for Islam, including building new mosques. Large sums have been lavished on the refurbishing of Shia religious shrines in an apparent effort to woo Iraqi Shias away from Shia opposition leaders. From 1974 to 1981, the Shia holy places in Karbala received $80 million, and in 1982—the year in which the fortunes of war turned against the Iraqi government and it had a particularly pressing need to assure Shia support—$48 million were allocated to Karbala and Najaf. The inner shrine of the Shia al-Haydariya mosque in Najaf was overlain with gold and silver leaf, and the two big Shia mosques in Karbala, home to the tombs of Imam Hussein and Imam Abbas, were given marble work, crystal chandeliers, power generators, and air conditioning.[54]

Iraqi Christians, who make up some 5 to 7 percent of the population, also enjoy freedom of worship under the protection of the state. The government officially recognizes fifteen Christian communities. Christian sects are, however, forbidden to proselytize among Muslims, although Muslims are allowed to do so among Christians. In 1980 and 1981, Iraqi Christians complained that government schools were obliging their children to attend classes in Islamic religion; according to an émigré Iraqi Christian interviewed by Middle East Watch, the complaints brought an end to the practice and it is not known to have recurred. According to Iraqi Assyrian émigrés interviewed by Middle East Watch, a number of Assyrian Christian churches in the northern mountain region of Iraq, some of them dating from the twelfth and thirteenth centuries, have been destroyed during the government's various campaigns against the Kurdish rebellion and the razing of villages that accompanied and followed these campaigns.[55] These sources believed that the government monitors closely the activities of the Assyrian Christian clergy because of its traditional identification with Assyrian nationalist sentiment. According to one Iraqi Assyrian émigré interviewed by Middle East Watch, the teaching of the Assyrian language, even in the precinct of churches, is forbidden, and Assyrian Christians who identify themselves as such suffer official discrimination. However, other Christians and those Assyrians who identify themselves as "Arab" seem to face no particular discrimination. In fact, many Muslim Iraqis consider Christians to be a favored minority under the Baath regime.

Until the mid-1940s Iraq had a Jewish population of over 120,000, including many prominent in business and the professions. All but a few thousand left in the early 1950s. Those who stayed suffered terrible persecution at the hands of the Baath party after it seized power in 1968. In an effort to establish itself as the standard-bearer of Arab nationalism, the Baath regime hung some fifteen Jews in 1969 and 1970 on charges of spying.[56] Others were arrested and tortured to death. In 1972, more Jews were arrested; twenty were murdered and sixteen disappeared.[57] According to a former state department official interviewed by Middle East Watch, in 1974 a Jewish family of some half dozen persons was slaughtered in its home in Baghdad by an arm of the Iraqi secret police.

Iraq's Jewish community now numbers no more than a few hundred. It is officially recognized and one small synagogue remains open in Baghdad. According to an American journalist who visited it in the summer of 1989, the synagogue is well kept. It receives some financial support from the Iraqi government and recently was given authorization to install an air-conditioning system.[58] The government appears, however, to draw a distinction between the Jewish religion, to which it accords official status and support, and Jews, who though no longer regularly subjected to arrest, torture, and killing, are barely tolerated. The American journalist was spat upon when she made inquiries in her attempt to locate the synagogue. She found members of the Jewish community living in abject poverty, denied the state welfare payments enjoyed by other Iraqis, prohibited from owning land, and barred from emigrating.[59]

Yazidis, a small sect of Kurds whose religion is a combination of paganism, Zoroastrianism, Christianity, and Islam, have also reportedly been persecuted from time to time though they enjoy governmental recognition. The Bahai faith is banned and adherence to it is punishable by imprisonment, or by death in the case of those found to return to it after having given it up.[60]

FREEDOM OF ASSOCIATION

The Iraqi Constitution establishes freedom of association in the same article and in the same manner as freedom of expression: what it gives with one hand it takes away with the other. Article 26 guarantees freedom to "form . . . political parties, unions and societies" but specifies that this freedom is to be exercised "in accordance with the aims of the Constitution and within the limits of the law." As in so many other cases, this constitutional restriction stands in contradiction to the provisions of the International Covenant on Civil and Political Rights, which in Article 22 provides that "everyone shall have the right to freedom of association with others" and stipulates that "no restrictions may be placed on the exercise of this right other than those which are prescribed by law and which are necessary in a democratic society in the interests of national security or public safety, public order, the protection of public health or morals or the protection of the rights and freedoms of others."

The Covenant notwithstanding, Iraq is a single-party state where only the Baath party and, currently, two small satellite Kurdish parties are allowed to operate.[61] Parties at the center of the political spectrum have long been banned. The Iraqi Communist party was driven underground in 1978 and later outlawed, and the two major Kurdish opposition parties, the Kurdish Democratic Party and the Patriotic Union of Kurdistan, are both banned.

The Iraqi General Federation of Trade Unions is the only labor association permitted.[62] It was established in 1987, after its predecessor, the Federation of Trade Unions, was summarily abolished. The abolition occurred on March 11, 1987, when, according to one scholar's account, President Saddam Hussein called in the leaders of the federation and startled them with the announcement that their union, the Labor Code of 1970, and the law on pensions and social security were to be abolished, and that henceforth workers were to put in twelve-hour days in the interest of increasing wartime production. "We say everybody works twelve hours per day and there would not be people that work eight hours," was the explanation offered by President Hussein.[63] The Iraqi General Federation of Trade Unions, like its predecessor, is "organically linked to the Baath party and required to promote party principles and policies among union members."[64]

Under the repealed Labor Code of 1970, industrial workers and others employed in state enterprises were permitted union membership. But under the new "Trade Union Organization Law" issued on June 2, 1987, union membership is open only to workers in private and mixed enterprises, not to employees of state enterprises, although in Iraq all heavy industry is state-owned.[65] Neither the Labor Code of 1970 nor that of 1987 recognized the right of collective bargaining. On this point and on several others, particularly the exclusion of public-sector workers from union membership, the International Labor Organization's Committee of Experts has found the Iraqi government to be in violation of ILO conventions.[66]

The right to strike is recognized in Iraqi law but denied in practice. According to the U.S. State Department, no strikes have been reported in Iraq for almost twenty years.[67] According to one organization, a strike did take place in Basra in 1979 in protest over wage cuts but was quickly put down by force.[68]

Foreign workers seem to enjoy even fewer protections, and in the case of Egyptians apparently almost none. During the 1980–88 war, more than a million Egyptian workers came to Iraq, mostly as industrial or agricultural laborers, to fill jobs left vacant by Iraqis mobilized for the war front. "The bullying of robed Egyptian workers around Baghdad airport by Iraqi officials has long been a common sight for travelers," according to a *New York Times* report.[69] In the fall of 1989, Egyptian newspapers began to report killings of Egyptian workers in Iraq. The Egyptian press has quoted some workers as saying that their Iraqi employers opened fire on them, that Iraqi banks had held up the transfer of their savings, and that Iraqi employers were refusing to pay their wages. One young worker was quoted as saying that he had been beaten and pressed into forced labor when he complained that he had not been paid for four months.[70] These reports are said to have set off panic among Egyptians and led to their mass departure from Iraq. Mistreatment of Egyptian workers also caused friction in relations between Cairo and Baghdad.

4

THE FORMS OF REPRESSION

In Iraq of the 1970s and 1980s, the victims of repression came from a broad range of groups—conservatives, liberals, non-Baathi Arab nationalists, Communists, Shias, Kurds, Assyrian Christians, Jews, students, intellectuals, military personnel, and even Baath party members and senior figures of the regime. Large numbers of journalists, writers, intellectuals, doctors, students, and academics, many of them Communists, were arrested, executed or disappeared in the late 1970s and early 1980s. Persons in fact or alleged to be of Iranian descent were deported in mass, and Shia Muslim fundamentalists and opposition figures were deported in large numbers or arrested, tortured, and executed from the late 1970s through the mid-1980s, by which time active Shia opposition in Iraq had been effectively crushed. Iraq's Kurds have periodically been subjected to large-scale and, since 1987, particularly severe repression.

Today most observers of the Iraqi scene judge the repression to have been so successful that, outside the Kurdish areas, virtually no known opposition remains. Those who have found it impossible to conform or to disguise their disagreement with the regime are either dead, in prison, or beyond the country's borders. Well over a million Iraqis live in exile, scattered in Iran, Turkey, Syria, other Arab countries, Western Europe, and the United States. As for those who remain, theirs is the common lot of citizens of police states: if they keep quiet, go about their business, avoid arousing suspicion, and show the proper degree of enthusiasm for the regime and its leader, they can expect to live in peace, benefit from the rewards that the regime dispenses, and perhaps even prosper. This chapter examines what has happened to those who have not conformed to Baath rule in Iraq.

ARBITRARY ARREST AND DETENTION

A panoply of laws theoretically provides full protection to the Iraqi citizens against arbitrary arrest and detention. Article 22 of the constitution provides that "no one may be arrested, detained, imprisoned or searched except in accordance with the provisions of the law." This requirement is repeated and amplified in Articles 92 through 120 of the Code of Criminal Procedure, which set out the rules for arrest, detention, and release on bail. An arrested person must, according to the law, be shown the warrant for his arrest and brought before the issuing authority; and he or she may not be held for more than 15 days without being brought to court or released.[1]

These provisions of Iraqi domestic law are reinforced by Article 9 of the International Covenant on Civil and Political Rights, which stipulates that "[n]o one shall be subjected to arbitrary arrest or detention." According to the Iraqi government, the protections afforded by the constitution and the Covenant remained in effect throughout Iraq's war with Iran.[2]

By most testimony, the procedural guarantees set out in Iraqi law are generally respected in common criminal cases.[3] In political and security cases, however, these guarantees appear to be uniformly disregarded. The various security police have the power to arrest and detain, or to take other arbitrary measures, at will, without warrant, charge, or bail, and without time limit. They can arrest in whatever manner they choose, and almost always do so in a manner that inspires a degree of terror. Political and security suspects have sometimes been taken away secretly without notice to family, friends, or colleagues, who then have had to make a desperate trek to security offices and prisons to locate them. Others have been taken away in front of family members or colleagues but with nothing said of their destination or the reason for their arrest. Vast numbers of Iraqis have been detained arbitrarily. Some have been released in a few days or months, only to be arrested again later; others have been tried and sentenced; and still others have disappeared or been killed in prison or held there indefinitely without trial. No one knows the number of political prisoners in Iraq. Estimates range from a few thousand to tens of thousands.[4]

Arbitrary arrest is a powerful tool for the repression of political dissent. The knowledge that the knock on the door could come at any hour is enough to inspire terror in most people. But it is only one, and in fact the most gentle, of those that the Iraqi regime is known to employ.

TORTURE

When he was released on October 18, 1983, after being held for 110 days in a Baghdad security prison without ever having been charged, Robert Spurling told U.S. diplomats that his treatment at the hands of his Iraqi jailers was "nothing" compared to that meted out to Iraqis and other Arabs he saw there. Spurling, a U.S. citizen, was then fifty and the technical director of the luxury Baghdad Novotel Hotel.[5] He was on the point of boarding a flight to Paris on the night of June 29–30, 1983, together with his Belgian wife and children, when he simply disappeared. Unbeknown to his family, he had been deftly diverted down a ramp where security agents and a car awaited him. Mrs. Spurling frantically sought the assistance of U.S. diplomatic representatives in Baghdad. More than a week passed before Iraqi authorities answered their inquires and acknowledged that Spurling was being held.[6] They never explained why he was detained.

Spurling later told U.S. officials that he was abducted, blindfolded, and driven to what he assumed to be the headquarters of the Baghdad security forces. There, he was interrogated and tortured repeatedly, pressed first to confess to spying and later simply to give information on others. "On July 6 and 23," he later testified, "I was given blows with a rubber truncheon on the soles of my feet, electric shocks were applied to my hands, feet, kidney region, genitals and above all to my ears, blows with the forearm to my head, four blows with a rubber truncheon on the upper part of my feet, two blows to the ears with boot heels, blows to the ears with cushions resembling boxing gloves and violent slaps."[7] Spurling was threatened with mutilation and was told that his wife and children had been arrested and would be mistreated unless he cooperated. (This was untrue; Mrs. Spurling remained in Baghdad throughout her husband's detention, and while Iraqi authorities encouraged her to leave they did not harass her.) Spurling was fed half portions for a time and then fed irregularly. On several occasions he was given spoiled and heavily salted food to induce nausea and thirst. More fortunate than most, he was given a cell to himself, which he shared only briefly with an Iraqi political prisoner, but the cell had an external temperature control which enabled his jailers alternately to make it very hot or very cold. And "time after time I had to listen to the cries and noises of other prisoners while they were being interrogated under torture."[8]

Because Spurling was a U.S. citizen at a time when the Iraqi government was looking to improve its relations with the United States, he was—as he himself stated—dealt with far more gently than others in his place of detention. The United States pressed the Iraqi government hard for access to Spurling. Before producing Spurling for his first meeting with U.S. diplomats, his Iraqi jailers gave him medical treatment for the wounds on his feet. At that meeting he obeyed their order to say that he was being well treated. But at his second meeting with U.S. representatives, Spurling defied these warnings and revealed that he had been tortured. According to a U.S. official present at the meeting, Spurling's revelation caused Iraqi officials acute embarrassment.[9] The United States immediately lodged vigorous diplomatic protests and demanded Spurling's release. After that he was well treated. When released several weeks later he was in relatively good shape, although scars on his feet were quite visible and were seen by U.S. diplomatic personnel in Baghdad.

Spurling was examined by an Amnesty International physician in Paris on October 25, 1983, one week after his release. His only problems then were digestive troubles, pains at the base of his spine and in his feet, lack of feeling in his right thumb, and difficulty in bending one finger.[10]

Peter Worth, a British civil engineer employed in Iraq, reported having been arrested, beaten, and tortured by electric shock in 1981. His reported offense was to have leaned against a wall at a construction project, accidentally causing a picture of Saddam Hussein to fall to the ground. Speaking of his ordeal, Worth later said: "I felt the . . . electric shock go through my arm, then other parts of my body, including my private parts." Worth said he signed a bogus confession to spying and was deported.[11]

Not so lucky as Peter Worth or Robert Spurling was Neji Bennour, reception manager at the Novotel Hotel, who was arrested a few weeks before Spurling. A Tunisian citizen, Bennour was dealt with in the manner accorded Iraqis and other Arabs. According to his later testimony, he was arrested while at work after having been tricked into going to the hotel's parking lot, where he was forced into the trunk of a car and driven to what he assumed was the security police headquarters in Baghdad. There he was beaten before being put into a cell jammed with more than two hundred other prisoners. He was held there for ten months. He later testified to Amnesty International that he was tortured repeatedly, some one hundred times by his count. He stated that he was given electric shocks on his ears, thumbs, little fingers, nipples, and between his big toes; beaten on the head and legs with a bare cable; repeatedly hit with fists and rubber truncheons, including on the soles of his feet and on the cervical, dorsal, and lumbar vertebrae for long periods; and kicked on the face, head, back, hands, legs, and feet.[12]

Bennour said that at first he was not even accused of spying; all the security police wanted was that he collaborate with them and denounce colleagues at work. In September 1983, over three months after his arrest, he signed a paper confessing to espionage and rape. Then torture ceased, and six months later, on April 2, 1984, without ever having been formally charged or tried, he was released.

When Bennour was examined by a doctor in Paris seventeen days later, he was found to have a variety of scars and to suffer from headaches, diminished hearing, some loss of vision, spinal pain, pains in the heels and feet, fatigue, and difficulty in breathing during exertion. He complained of rapid heartbeat in the evenings, nightmares and acute anxiety.[13]

The Iraqi government consistently denies all charges that its officials engage in torture. In the cases of Spurling and Bennour, an Iraqi official stated in a letter to Amnesty International that the two men had been "arrested in accordance with regulations [and] were not subject to any form of torture during their detention." The official added: "We take this opportunity to confirm what we have demonstrated before, that there is no torture in Iraq."[14]

Iraqi spokesmen invariably reply to reports of torture by citing a battery of legal provisions—Article 22 of the Iraqi Constitution, which prohibits physical or psychological torture;[15] Chapter III of the 1969 Penal Code, which also prohibits torture; Article 323 of the Code of Criminal Procedure, which prohibits the use of unlawful means to obtain a confession; Article 333 of the Penal Code, which stipulates that any government employee who tortures or orders torture is to be punished by imprisonment; and Article 322, of the Penal Code which prohibits government employees from taking advantage of their position to treat any person harshly or in a manner detrimental to his honor or dignity or to cause him physical pain. Iraqi spokesmen point out that their government has announced its voluntary compliance with the provisions of the United Nations Declaration on the Protection of all Persons from Being Subjected to Torture and other Cruel, Inhuman or Degrading Treatment or Punishment[16] and is considering accession to the Convention against Torture and Other Cruel, Inhuman or Degrading Treatment or Punishment.[17]

Anyone who has been tortured, Iraqi spokesmen add, is entitled under the law to institute criminal proceedings against the torturer. Iraq told the U.N. Human Rights Committee in 1986 that "[t]he party responsible for ordering and carrying out the torture, even if it were a governmental body, would be duly sentenced to the prescribed penalty and would be held liable for any incapacity or damages resulting from the offense." [18] Iraqi officials have said that persons have been found guilty of assault on prisoners and have been punished, but the government has refused to substantiate this claim, and in no instance is anyone known to have filed suit in Iraqi courts for damages from torture. [19]

But while vociferously denying charges of torture, Iraq has never allowed a private human rights group or United Nations body to visit its prisons and to interview prisoners or victims of torture. In the meantime, voluminous reports of torture committed over the years by Iraqi jailers continue to emerge—reports from victims of torture, from relatives of victims and from others, corroborated in many cases by medical evidence.

Nabil Jamil al-Janabi, an Iraqi poet living in exile in London, recently gave a public account of the torture he suffered at the security-force headquarters in Baghdad after his arrest in March 1976. Janabi, an Arab Iraqi, had read one of his poems to an assembly of Kurds at Sinjar, in western Mosul province. He was arrested and driven to Baghdad:

> I was taken by two very big gunmen into a single, cold, dark cell with no bedding. . . . The door of the cell was opened at 3 a.m. They took me out, blindfolded, to an unknown place. . . . They started torturing me by attaching one end of an electric wire to my left big toe and the other end to my penis. They put the power on and I lost consciousness for about an hour, then they repeated this with the electric wire attached to my right foot. Again I passed out. While I lay half dead on the floor they tried to revive me by torturing me with cigarettes and steel rods. When I regained consciousness again, they tied my head and both legs together and put me into a tyre. They started to spin it; two men on either side kept spinning me round and round. In addition to all this, I was completely naked, they'd taken off my pants. Then they started to beat me. Two men were beating me with electric rods, hitting my testicles. [20]

Nabil al-Janabi reported that he signed a piece of paper without knowing what was on it, was sent to a "revolutionary court" where he was tried without the assistance of a defense attorney, and was sentenced to five years in prison for publishing a poem "calculated to incite people to act against the government." [21] After being released, he was arrested again in 1982, held for two weeks and again tortured. He fled Iraq for Britain in 1983. The physician who examined him there stated:

Mr. Jamil suffers from hypertension, ischaemic heart disease and diabetes mellitus. He also appears to have a lumbo-sacral prolapsed intervertebral disc and problems with various joints, almost certainly related to the torture to which he has been subjected. . . . Mr. Jamil has been subjected to gross brutality and is now in a somewhat precarious state of health.[22]

Many Iraqi torture victims do not live to tell their story. Ahmed Mattar, another Iraqi poet living in exile in London, wrote these lines in memory of a friend who died under torture in Iraq.

> They imprisoned him
> before they charged him
> They tortured him
> before they interrogated him
> They stubbed out cigarettes in his eyes
> and held up some pictures in front of him
> Say whose faces are these
> He said: I do not see
> They cut off his lips
> and demanded that he name
> those "they" had recruited
> He said nothing
> and when they failed to make him talk
> they hanged him.
> A month later they cleared him
> They realized the young man
> was not the one they really wanted
> but his brother. . . .[23]

Of course, of those who survive torture in Iraq's prisons, only a relatively few reach the West, and not all of those are willing to speak of their ordeal. One who did agree to give testimony to Middle East Watch, a former lecturer at Baghdad University, insisted on anonymity in order to protect relatives still in Iraq.

They came to my house in Baghdad in December 1979 just after midnight. They broke down the door, searched the house, blindfolded and handcuffed me, hit me with a rubber truncheon and took me to Baghdad security headquarters. There I was taken to the third floor, my clothes were taken from me and I was given a traditional Iraqi robe. I was then told: "We have documents showing that you are one of the leaders of the Dawa party." When I denied it they said, "We give you a few minutes to think it over. If you don't confess we will torture you." I asked them to show me the documents; they replied they would do that once I confessed. After that for 35 days they tortured me every day or every other day. I was beaten on the feet and hung for long periods of time by my arms from ropes anchored in the ceiling; they debated whether to hang me from my arms tied behind my back, but I was much heavier then and they realized that if they did that the bones in my arms and shoulders would break. When they weren't torturing me they kept me in a cell with over 100 other people, with no sanitation facilities. At the end of 35 days they said they would let me go if I joined the Baath party. I refused but they released me anyway, but everyday a security officer came to my house to question me. Colleagues at the University warned me that I was going to be arrested again, so at the beginning of March 1980 I fled the country. [London, September 1989]

In a report issued in 1981, Amnesty International summarized the testimony of fifteen Iraqi exiles—twelve men and three women—who had been tortured in Iraq in the preceding years. One of them, Burhan al-Shawi, a twenty-four-year-old journalist and writer who was arrested in Baghdad in November 1978 and fled Iraq in May 1979, agreed to have his name used in the account he gave. Amnesty reported:

During the first two days he was taken to different rooms and beaten with fists, rods and a whip. . . . In one room he was caressed and sexually fondled, before being taken out and beaten and kicked. The torture then became more systematic, taking place every one or two hours. His head was whipped and beaten so hard that he lost consciousness. . . . After regaining consciousness on one occasion he was aware that his trousers had been removed and realized that he had been raped. He was then made to sit on a cold bottle-like object which was forced up his rectum. He was also burned with a hard object about the size of a pencil.[24]

Burhan al-Shawi and the fourteen other torture victims who gave personal testimony were examined by physicians in London who in all cases "found that the tortures described were consistent with the subsequent symptoms and the signs found during the physical examination."[25]

For sheer horror, nothing is likely to surpass the nightmarish scene described by an Iraqi mother who went to the Baghdad morgue to collect her son's body in September 1982. The boy was arrested in December 1981 and held without charge or trial, and without his family knowing his whereabouts. Here is an excerpt of the woman's testimony:

> I looked around and saw 9 bodies stretched out on the floor with him
> . . . but my son was in a chair form . . . that is a sitting form, not
> sleeping or stretched. He had blood all over him and his body was very
> eaten away and bleeding. I looked at the others stretched out on the floor
> alongside him . . . all burnt . . . I don't know with what . . . another's
> body carried the marks of a hot domestic iron all over his head to his
> feet. . . . At the mortuary the bodies were on the floor . . . one of them
> had his chest cut lengthwise into three sections . . . from the neck to the
> bottom of the chest was slit with what must have been a knife and the
> flesh looked white and roasted as if cooked. . . . Another had his legs
> axed with an axe . . . his arms were also axed. One of them had his eyes
> gouged out and his nose and ears cut off. . . . One of them looked
> hanged . . . his neck was long . . . his tongue was hanging out and the
> fresh blood was oozing out of his mouth.[26]

The woman testified that "corpses were returned [to the families] in this horrifying manner" for about a month and a half, but later the practice stopped and the authorities began giving out only death certificates.[27]

Large numbers of persons have unquestionably died under torture in Iraq over the past two decades. Each year there have been reports of dozens—sometimes hundreds—of deaths, with bodies of victims at times left in the street or returned to families bearing marks of torture: eyes gouged out, fingernails missing, genitals cut off, and terrible wounds and burns. The brazenness of Iraqi authorities in returning bodies bearing clear evidence of torture is remarkable. Governments that engage in torture often go to great lengths to hide what they have done by burying or destroying the bodies of those tortured to death. A government so savage as to flaunt its crimes obviously wants to strike terror in the hearts of its citizens and to inflict gratuitous pain on the families of the victims.

Torture has been reportedly used not only against men and women but also against children, either to obtain information from them, to punish them for acts of opposition, or to punish their parents. Kurdish children have been among the victims of detention and torture. A former Baghdad University student, arrested as a sympathizer of the outlawed Kurdish Democratic Party and released in April 1985 after having been tortured, reported that his mother, aged seventy-three, three brothers, three sisters, and five of their children between the ages of five and thirteen were arrested, beaten, and subjected to electric shocks. This witness testified, "Infant children are kept in [the] detention center together with their parents. Usually they keep such children in a separate cell next to [the] mother in order to force [the] parent to confess. I saw a five-month-old baby screaming in this state."[28]

In September and October 1985, some 300 Kurdish children and teenagers were reportedly arrested in Suleimanieh.[29] The bodies of three children were reportedly found afterward on the outskirts of the city, bloodstained and bearing the marks of torture. Some of these children were transferred to a security prison in Baghdad, according to the testimony of a detainee released at the end of 1985, who described in these terms what he saw:

Each hour, security men opened the door and chose 3 to 5 of the prisoners—children or men—and removed them for torture. Later, their tortured bodies were thrown back into the cell. They were often bleeding and carried obvious signs of whipping and electric shocks. . . . At midnight, the security men took another three of the children, but because they were so savagely treated they were taken from the cell to a military hospital. It was clear that the security authorities did not wish them to die like this. However when their wounds healed they were returned to the cell. Some children tried to sleep on the floor. A child who had been in the hospital lay down and finally, we thought, fell asleep. But . . . we knew he was dead. . . . When I was released, there were still some children in our cell. I don't know what happened to the others.[30]

In January 1987, it was reported that twenty-nine of these children had been executed and their bodies returned to their families, some with eyes gouged out and other marks of torture.[31] Although the Iraqi government vehemently denied these reports, the European Parliament deemed them sufficiently credible to speak out about them. In its resolution "on the detention and torture of children in Iraq," the European Parliament condemned "these crimes which disgrace the government which perpetrates them" and appealed for "the immediate release of all the children and young people detained on the basis of political activities undertaken by their parents or relations."[32]

That torture is used routinely as a method of political repression in Iraq, and that it frequently involves acts of great savagery, is credited by a wide range of nongovernmental human rights groups as well as the U.S. State Department.[33] According to knowledgeable U.S. officials interviewed by Middle East Watch, torture is not limited to political and security prisoners; while anyone arrested for these offenses can expect to be tortured, criminal suspects are also frequently tortured and almost always subjected to brutal treatment, at least in the early stages of detention.

POLITICAL KILLING

In May 1978, Soviet sources leaked to the international media that as many as forty Iraqi Communists had been executed and some thousand members of the Iraqi Communist party had been arrested. In June, Iraqi officials acknowledged that twenty-one Communists had been executed, on the charge of forming secret cells inside the army.[34] What the Iraqi announcement did not reveal was that the twenty-one executed soldiers could hardly have been considered a serious threat: they had been held in prison since 1975, all but three or four of them were from the noncommissioned ranks, and the rest were junior officers. Saddam Hussein explained why they were executed in an interview with *Newsweek* magazine's Arnaud de Borchgrave published on July 17, 1978, the tenth anniversary of the Baath party's seizure of power. The executions, he said, had been carried out after the Soviet ambassador had made an appeal for clemency. They were, the Iraqi leader added, intended as a warning to Moscow against meddling in Iraq's internal affairs.

Political killing has been a hallmark of the Baath regime in Iraq from the beginning. In one of its first moves after seizing power in 1968, the regime launched a series of political trials, on accusations ranging from spying for Israel, the United States and Iran to intending to overthrow the regime and corruption. On January 26, 1969, sixteen persons, ten of them Jews, were sentenced to death. The next day fourteen of the condemned were publicly hanged in Baghdad and Basra, with a crowd estimated at between one-hundre-fifty thousand and five hundred thousand brought out to witness the event in Baghdad and to hear speeches by President Ahmad Hassan al-Bakr and other senior officials.[35] Additional trials and executions were officially announced in February, April, May, August, September, and November 1969. After the January executions, most of the victims were Muslims and Christians, although a few Jews were occasionally thrown in, perhaps to lend verisimilitude to charges that former high officials had been guilty of spying for Israel. For example, Izra Naji Zilkha, a Jewish merchant in Baghdad, was accused of having formed a political organization with the intent of overthrowing the government and establishing another that would make peace between Iraq and Israel.[36] In January 1970 it was announced that a new conspiracy had been uncovered and thirty-seven men and women were executed; at least eighty-six executions were officially announced in the course of the year.[37] Hundreds of others were imprisoned.

The next major bloodletting was an internal one, involving senior members of the regime and the Baath party. It came in July 1973, after Nadhim Kzar, the regime's first chief of Internal State Security with the reputation of a ruthless and sadistic torturer, made a bungled attempt to assassinate President al-Bakr and other top figures. Kzar and thirty-five others were executed after a summary trial by a tribunal composed exclusively of members of the Revolutionary Command Council. In the words of one historian, these executions "paved the way for the unquestioned dominance of . . . al-Baqr and Husayn." [38]

Further purges marked Saddam Hussein's takeover from al-Bakr in July 1979. As described in chapter 2, less than two weeks after he assumed the presidency, Hussein announced the discovery of a plot to overthrow the regime. Twenty-two senior officials, among them five members of the Revolutionary Command Council, were executed after summary trial.[39] Many foreign observers doubted whether a plot existed, believing instead that the executions were intended to clear the scene of actual or potential opponents of the new president.

In 1980 two former senior regime figures were killed. In April, former foreign minister and RCC member Abdul Karim al-Shaikhly was murdered in Baghdad. Al-Shaikhly had been Iraqi ambassador to the United Nations until 1978 when he was summoned home and sentenced to six years in prison on charges of conspiracy against the state. Another former foreign minister and RCC member, Murtada Saad Abdul Baqi, was reportedly executed in Baghdad in June 1980. Abdul Baqi had been ambassador to the USSR until July 1979 when he was recalled to Baghdad and put under house arrest.

The killing of both men was reportedly connected to the executions of the summer of 1979.[40] In November 1982 the Iraqi News Agency reported the execution of Health Minister Dr. Riyadh Ibrahim Hussein. It was rumored that Dr. Hussein, had been overheard to say at a party that President Saddam Hussein should step down, but the officially announced reason for his execution was that he had imported medicine that had killed people and was "a traitor." According to various unconfirmed reports, Dr. Hussein's body was sent to his wife chopped into pieces after she personally pleaded with President Saddam Hussein that he be freed and allowed to return home.[41]

Repeated purges and executions of senior army officers were reported during the Iran-Iraq War. Potential rivals or insubordinates at the top of the military command were retired or died in suspicious circumstances. Former President al-Bakr was killed in an automobile accident in 1983, an event that many found strangely coincidental with wartime dissatisfaction over Saddam Hussein's rule and muted calls for al-Bakr's reinstatement as president. From 1985 to 1987, between eighteen and twenty senior officials, among them the mayor of Baghdad, were reportedly executed on charges of "corruption."[42] In August and September 1988, Generals Dhaffer Abdul Rashid and Salman Shuja, both successful and popular military commanders, were killed in separate helicopter crashes.[43] In January 1989, fourteen Baath party members and army officers were reportedly executed on suspicion of plotting a coup.[44] In June 1989, yet another helicopter crash took the life of Defense Minister Adnan Khairallah Talfah, Saddam Hussein's brother-in-law and for years one of his closest associates. Opinions differ on whether Khairallah's death was accidental or arranged, but it was widely reported that he and Saddam Hussein had fallen out over Hussein's decision at the beginning of the year to take a second wife.

If senior officials of the regime have been among those liquidated, it is the regime's opponents that have been the main object of political killing. Foremost among these have been Iraqi Communists, Shia religious leaders and Kurds.

The repressive pro-Western rule of the Iraqi monarchy in the years following World War II created fertile ground for the growth of the Communist party. Even though the Iraqi Communist party was obliged to operate clandestinely under the monarchy, it flourished and became one of the largest in the Arab world. It played an important role in the turbulent decade between the overthrow of the monarchy in 1958 and the Baath party's seizure of power in 1968. In 1973 the Baath brought the Communists into a "National Progressive Front" and gave them two ministerial portfolios.[45] After the Baath and the Communists fell out in 1978, the regime pursued Iraqi Communists relentlessly, killing hundreds and imprisoning thousands, and even pursuing some who escaped abroad. As earlier noted, the killing of several Iraqi Communists in Aden in 1979 brought about the rupture of relations between Iraq and South Yemen.

Intellectuals and the medical profession bore the brunt of this repression, as many Iraqi journalists, writers, teachers, and doctors belonged to or were affiliated with the Communist party. According to émigré sources, between 1978 and 1980 the Baath regime effectively wiped out the Iraqi Communist party, though executions of small numbers of Iraqi Communists have continued throughout the 1980s.[46]

Shia opposition to the Baath regime reached a boiling point in the late 1970s and early 1980s, fired in part by the rise to power of Ayatollah Khomeini in Iran and in part by the Iraqi regime's detention and execution of prominent members of the Shia clergy. In February and June 1979, there was widespread rioting in Karbala and Najaf, Iraqi cities holy to the Shia, and in the mainly Shia Baghdad shantytown of al-Thawra. In response the Iraqi government reportedly executed some twenty Shias, including a number of religious scholars.[47] After further riots in December 1979, Shia Ayatollah Baqr al-Sadr was arrested. Al-Sadr, a prolific writer and the leading Iraqi Shia intellectual of his day, was accused of being the leader of the outlawed Shia al-Dawa organization. Early in 1980, he and his sister, Bint al-Huda, were executed on charges of plotting with Iran against Iraq.[48]

During the early years of the Iran-Iraq War, the Iraqi government directed particularly savage acts of repression at the prominent Shia al-Hakim family, whose members had distinguished themselves for generations in theology, law, medicine, and science. Before the outbreak of the war, one family member, Mohammed Baqr al-Hakim, fled Iraq for Tehran, where he made regular radio broadcasts attacking the Iraqi regime and calling for Iraqi Shias to rise up against it. He was also said to have been active in organizing and directing the operations of al-Dawa. At the beginning of May 1983, Iraqi authorities arrested some eighty to ninety male members of the al-Hakim family, ranging in age from nine to eighty, and on May 13 six were executed. Mohammed Hussein al-Hakim, one of the arrested family members and a man in his seventies, was forced to witness the executions.

In shock, traumatized and terrified [Mohammed Hussein al-Hakim] fainted. He was then put in a cell alone for ten days, mistreated and left without care, his eyes bandaged shut. Several days later he was taken to

Baghdad international airport . . . where he was put on an Iraqi Airlines flight for Istanbul. Immediately before boarding the plane he was given $200 and was ordered to continue his trip to Tehran where he was to deliver the following message of warning to Mohammed Baqr al-Hakim: "Mohammed Baqr Hakim must cease his activities against the Iraqi regime, otherwise all the other members of his family will be executed." [49]

Iraqi authorities ordered Mohammed Hussein al-Hakim to return to Baghdad once he had completed his mission, and they threatened to execute his three sons—also taken hostage—if he failed to do so. In Tehran, Mohammed Hussein al-Hakim went insane and died. On March 5, 1985, the Iraqi government executed his three sons and seven other members of the al-Hakim family. [50] According to al-Hakim family sources, some six others have since been killed or died while in detention and fifty-three remain jailed. In November 1987, as noted, Iraqi agents lured another prominent member of the family, Mahdi al-Hakim, from his London exile to Khartoum and there shot him dead. [51]

Observers of the Iraqi scene have repeatedly pointed out that in the war with Iran, most of Iraq's front line troops—and casualties—were Shias, and that by standing with the regime and fighting, the Shias saved it. Why the majority of Iraqi Shias remained loyal is a subject of much conjecture, however, since Shias were executed by the regime in large numbers during the war. In July 1981, twelve Shia officers and two hundred Shias from other ranks were reportedly executed by firing squads, allegedly for planning attempts on Saddam Hussein's life. [52] Shias suspected of membership in al-Dawa and other banned Shia organizations were rounded up in large numbers, and six hundred are estimated to have been executed in 1984 alone. [53] Most of the forty thousand or so soldiers who deserted are believed to have been Shias. According to expert testimony, soldiers suspected of desertion were shot on the spot when intercepted at military roadblocks, without being charged or tried. Many deserters were known to have fled to the marshlands of southeastern Iraq. According to an academic specialist on Iraq interviewed by Middle East Watch who requested anonymity, Iraqi helicopter gunships raked these areas with indiscriminate gunfire on several occasions, killing all in their path, Marsh Arabs as well as deserters.

Although Iraqi Shias have unquestionably suffered grievously at the hands of their government, Iraqi Kurds have borne the brunt of Iraqi repression before, during, and since the war. This chapter examines only the political killing of Kurds; other aspects of the Kurdish question are addressed in chapter 5. Kurds have been regularly killed in large numbers in Iraq for over a decade. According to Amnesty International and other groups:

From 1976 throughout 1978, more than two hundred Kurds were reportedly executed in Mosul prison, fifty-three of them in one night late in June or early in July 1977. None had access to a lawyer of their choosing or to an open trial or appeal.[54]

In 1979 executions of an undetermined number of members of illegal Kurdish parties were reported. In February and March 1979 twelve Kurds were reportedly executed in Mosul prison.[55]

In 1980 twenty Kurds were reportedly sentenced to death by a special court in Kirkuk; six were executed.[56]

In 1981 twenty-seven members of the outlawed Patriotic Union of Kurdistan (PUK), one of the two major opposition parties, were reportedly sentenced to death and fourteen were executed. Another one-hundred-forty supporters and members of the PUK were reportedly executed in Baghdad's Abu Ghraib prison at the end of September 1981.[57]

In 1982 ten PUK members were reportedly executed after trial by a special court in Kirkuk.[58]

In 1983 two of Mulla Mustapha Barzani's sons, Loqman and Sabra, were executed, reportedly along with fifteen other members of the Barzani clan, in reprisal for assistance given by their brother Masoud to Iranian forces in capturing the Iraqi Kurdish border town of Hajj Umran. Ubaidullah Barzani, another of Mulla Mustapha's sons, was reportedly executed in 1981 following a disagreement with President Saddam Hussein during a meeting in Baghdad.[59]

In March 1984 twenty-four young Kurds were executed in Suleimanieh, allegedly for desertion and draft dodging.[60] Fifteen to twenty others were reportedly killed and an unknown number of others wounded when security forces opened fire on a demonstration of students opposing summer service in the People's Militia.[61]

On March 31, 1985, thirteen members of the Kurdistan Popular Democratic Party were reportedly executed after having each been sentenced by a revolutionary court in 1984 to fifteen years' imprisonment. Another sixty prisoners were reportedly executed in Baghdad's Abu Ghraib prison in the first week of November 1985, among them Kurds belonging to the Kurdish Socialist Party and the Kurdish Democratic Party.[62]

Ten Kurds were reportedly executed in Suleimanieh by Iraqi security forces on October 14, 1985, in reprisal for the killing of two Iraqi officers earlier in the day. The ten were reportedly rounded up and shot outside a public bath. Iraqi forces also then razed a number of houses.[63] In 1986 forty-four Kurds were reportedly executed or sentenced to death in Iraq for political offenses.[64]

In 1987, the last full year of the Iran-Iraq War, the Iraqi government engaged in a frenzy of executions in Kurdish areas. On November 11, between one hundred and one-hundred-fifty Kurds of all ages were reported killed after house-to-house searches and bombardment of the village of Jiman in Kirkuk province. Between November 14 and 18, thirty-two Kurds from the town of Shaqlawa in Arbil province were reportedly executed by firing squad in the city of Arbil, in reprisal for an earlier Kurdish guerrilla attack on Iraqi soldiers. Their homes were also reportedly razed. Also on November 18, assistant veterinary surgeon Abdul Aziz Abdullah Othman, a member of the Kurdish Popular Democratic Party, was reportedly executed in Baghdad's Abu Ghraib prison and his body returned to his family. Thirty-one Kurds said to be sympathizers of the Kurdish Democratic Party were reportedly executed by firing squad in three separate incidents on November 18, December 10, and December 28; five were reportedly under the age of eighteen. Finally, on December 30 and 31, more than one-hundred-fifty political prisoners—Kurds, Arabs, and Turcomans—were reportedly executed in Baghdad's Abu Ghraib prison. Some were secondary school students.[65]

These previously published accounts should by no means be taken as comprehensive. From 1986 to 1988 summary executions in reprisal for Kurdish guerrilla attacks on Iraqi military or civilian personnel were commonplace in Kurdish regions of Iraq. Here is an account given to Middle East Watch of one such incident witnessed by a former Iraqi official who was in Arbil, the capital of the Kurdish Autonomous Region, on the day it occurred:

I was in Arbil when the governor was shot—only shot, not killed—in 1986. Three hours after the attempted assassination, in the Ronaky quarter, five young people between the ages of fourteen and nineteen were publicly executed in front of a crowd. I was there because the government rounded up government employees and told them to attend. I was horrified by what I saw. One of the young people was asked if he had anything to say but when he tried to speak he was told to shut up. I was too far away to see if the five had been beaten but others told me that their faces looked beaten. After that they were shot.

The same individual testified that he witnessed two other reprisal executions in Arbil:

> In November 1987, following the attempted assassination of a security official in Arbil, three young people between the ages of 14 and 17 were executed in the Shorsh quarter. The executions were announced by loudspeakers and people were ordered to attend. On July 2, 1988, in the Mohaltarab quarter of Arbil, a woman teacher who was a government informer was killed. Security officers brought a high school teacher from the jail and executed him with the pistol with which the woman was killed.

Some killings are said to have been disguised as natural deaths. According to testimony given to Middle East Watch by a former employee of the Arbil Teaching Hospital now in exile, a senior physician there regularly signed false death certificates during 1986 and 1987. While acknowledging privately that the dead had been executed in jails, the senior physician wrote out certificates attesting that they had died of heart attacks or other natural causes. These cases were considered "top secret" and the employee was cautioned against ever revealing them. According to this testimony, some twenty to twenty-five such certificates were issued per month at the Arbil Teaching Hospital during 1987 and 1988.

Since 1980 a number of political opponents have been reportedly poisoned. In May of that year, two Iraqis who reached London after detention in Iraq were examined by doctors and found to be suffering from poisoning by thallium, a heavy metal used in commercial rat poison which is odorless, colorless, and tasteless. One, Majidi Jehad, testified before dying that he believed the poison had been given him in an orange-juice drink he was offered at the Baghdad police station where he went to pick up his passport.[66] In another case, the British journal *New Scientist* reported:

> Shawkat A. Akrawi, a consulting industrial chemist who graduated from Leeds University, managed to "smuggle" a telephone call from a Baghdad hospital to a *New Scientist* contact. Speaking in Kurdish, he said: "The accident they arranged didn't kill me, so they gave me thallium in the hospital where I am being treated. Say goodbye to everybody." The line was then cut off.[67]

Some forty opposition Kurds were reportedly poisoned in separate incidents late in 1987.[68] One of them, Sami Shoresh, a Kurdish poet and writer,
gave the following account to Middle East Watch:

I was working in radio in the Kurdish Information Center in the liberated
area from 1980 to 1987. On November 24, 1987 (when I was 35)] I went
to the Merga area to write a story about the battle. I was with Dr. Mahmoud Othman, Adnan al-Mufti and Mustafa Mahmoud and a group of
others. We had lunch there and a yoghurt drink. About an hour after the
lunch one of the men said he felt ill, and he fell down. We took him to a
clinic but he began vomiting and became paralyzed and died. Then another man fell ill, and then a third; both died. Then we all went to a
hospital in the liberated area and were examined by a doctor who told us
we had been poisoned but that he did not have any medicine to treat us.
That was the day after the lunch and I didn't have any symptoms yet, but
the next morning I developed pain in my stomach and legs. My colleagues Dr. Othman, Adnan al-Mufti and Mustafa Mahmoud had the
same symptoms. We were sent to a hospital in Iran, a journey of three
days' and two nights' very difficult travel. We became very ill. The pains
in my stomach and legs became worse, I couldn't eat and my hair began
to fall out. . . . I felt constantly dizzy. Adnan and Mustafa and I were
taken to a hospital in Tehran run by the Kurdish Democratic Party and a
doctor there diagnosed it as thallium poisoning but said there was no
medicine for it in Iran. Someone from the U.N. visited us, and he
brought a German doctor to examine us who said our condition was very
bad and our prospect to live was poor if we didn't go quickly to Europe
for treatment. We were given travel documents but the Iranians would
not let us leave right away. They held us for another 25 days so that we
would be even more sick and die in Europe and in that way create bad
propaganda against Iraq. When I got to London I couldn't speak or walk.
We were treated at London Bridge Hospital. I stayed there three weeks
and so did Adnan; Mustafa was there two months and had to have an
operation for swelling of the liver. Now I am alright except that I tire
easily, after about a half hour walking.

An Amnesty International consulting physician who examined Sami Shoresh, Adnan al-Mufti, and Mustafa Mahmoud in London confirmed that they
were suffering from acute thallium poisoning.[69] When Amnesty's report on
their poisoning was published, the Iraqi ambassador in London issued a vo-

ciferous denial. Ambassador Mohammed al-Mashat declared that the report was "part of a series of fabrications being formulated by [Amnesty international] at a time when it has failed to expose to public opinion the vicious crimes being committed by the Iranian regime and its ally the Zionist entity." [70]

Persons other than Kurds have also been victims of thallium poisoning. In January 1988, Abdullah Rahim Sahrif Ali, an Iraqi who ran a printing house in London and who was said to be an agent of the Iraqi government, died of thallium poisoning. Ali died after dining with three Iraqi "businessmen" who flew from Baghdad to London for little more than a day and were not known to have transacted any business other than their meeting with him. [71] According to several sources in London, Ali had been ordered to return to Baghdad but had delayed doing so.

In yet another case in which the victim was interviewed by Middle East Watch and requested anonymity, thallium poisoning was used against an Arab businessman employed in the West by a multinational firm and sent to Baghdad in 1988. This individual's relations with Iraq had been mildly troubled by past business dealings; he felt some anxiety about making the trip but thought that his position together with the fact that he was a citizen of an Arab state with which Iraq desired to remain on good terms would afford adequate protection. Shortly after leaving Baghdad, this individual, until then in excellent health, was stricken with nausea, partial paralysis, and nervous disorders. He was diagnosed in Europe as having been poisoned by thallium; the diagnosing physician placed the poisoning precisely during the period of his stay in Baghdad. After treatment and six months of painful convalescence he recovered. He had received only a relatively small dose of the poison, evidently not intended to kill but to sicken and terrorize.

Among others who have frequently fallen afoul of the Iraqi regime are Assyrians and Turcomans. In February 1982, twenty-seven Turcomans were reportedly executed in the village of Tiss'een near Kirkuk. [72] In February 1985, three Assyrians—Yousef Toma Zibari, Youkhana Esho Shlimon, and Youbert Benyamin—were executed. Replying to a communication by Amnesty International, the Iraqi government confirmed these executions and accused the three of "having committed the crime of creating a hostile and separatist movement aimed at threatening the independence and unity of Iraq. . . . They transported weapons and carried out acts of sabotage." [73]

It is worth repeating that this catalog of reports of political killing in Iraq makes no claim to being complete. A full listing would be beyond the scope of this book and would, in any case, be virtually impossible to compile. Many cases of political killing have almost certainly gone unreported. As pointed out in the introduction, the crushing of the Kurdish insurgency following the end of the Iran-Iraq War has closed off one of the main avenues for transmitting information on political killing and other major human rights violations from Iraq. This, together with the severe restrictions the Iraqi regime places on travel abroad by its citizens, the frightening penalties it puts on the transmission of information, and its consistent refusal to allow any U.N. or private body to investigate, assures that much remains hidden and prevents verification of a great deal that does come to light. Yet there can be no doubt that political killing has occurred on a massive scale in Iraq over the past two decades. Despite the dearth of specific information over the past year or so, there is no reason to believe that the basic pattern of Iraqi government behavior in this regard has changed.

DISAPPEARANCE

When Dr. Hussain Shahristani and Dr. Jaafar Dhia Jaafar disappeared after being arrested by security police in Baghdad in 1979 and 1980, there was an international outcry. Both were internationally known scientists, and their scientific colleagues in the United States and Western Europe promptly spoke out in their defense.

Dr. Shahristani was director of research at the Iraqi Atomic Energy Commission when he was arrested on December 9, 1979. Despite the many appeals made on his behalf, the Iraqi government never divulged the reason for his arrest. Because Dr. Shahristani was a member of a leading Iraqi Shia family, it was speculated that he may have been suspected of links with the outlawed al-Dawa organization; but a Somali national who reportedly shared a cell with him at one point later related that the scientist believed he was arrested for refusing to develop a nuclear bomb with the reactor that Iraq had bought from France in the mid-1970s.[74]

There have been conflicting reports about what happened to Dr. Shahristani. He is said to have been seen in January 1980 in a military hospital in Baghdad in poor physical condition as a result of torture.[75] Iraqi scientists who escaped from Iraq in 1981 reportedly spoke of him as "the late Dr.

Shahristani."[76] But according to another report, a death sentence issued against him after a closed trial in 1980 was commuted to life imprisonment.[77] Dr. Jaafar Dhia Jaafar was the head of the Experimental Physics Department of the Iraqi Atomic Energy Commission. He was arrested in February 1980 after reportedly having sent a letter to President Saddam Hussein on the subject of Dr. Shahristani's arrest. Nothing has been heard of Dr. Jaafar since his arrest.

On December 11, 1984, following the resumption of diplomatic relations between the United States and Iraq, the chairman of the National Academy of Sciences Human Rights Committee, Eliot Stellar, wrote to Iraqi ambassador Nizar Hamdoon asking for information about the two scientists. In a letter dated July 11, 1985, the Iraqi ambassador replied that "Dr. Husain al-Shahristani and Dr. Ja'afar Dhia Ja'afer were released after receiving a PARDON [a] long time ago, and they are free at present."[78]

Although neither Dr. Shahristani nor Dr. Jaafar have been heard from directly since their arrests, recent indirect information suggests that both are alive but still in prison.

A rather ironic case of disappearance that received high-level attention was that of Mohammed al-Jabiri, Iraq's ambassador to Spain and chief delegate to the session of the United Nations Human Rights Commission in Geneva held in 1980. Iraq's delegates to the commission have a well-earned reputation for seeking to thwart rather than to promote human rights initiatives, even when the initiatives in question do not directly affect their country. But when, during the commission's 1980 session, Western delegates launched an effort to set up a working group on disappearances to deal with the massive disappearances then taking place in Argentina, they found Ambassador al-Jabiri genuinely sympathetic.[79] To their surprise, he played a helpful role in efforts undertaken that year to bring into being a strong, effective working group on disappearances, and he lobbied energetically and successfully for it with other Third World delegates.

When the commission approved the creation of the Working Group on Enforced or Involuntary Disappearances, Ambassador al-Jabiri was elected its chairman in recognition of his contribution. Whereupon, he was called back to Baghdad and disappeared. The director of the U.N. Human Rights Division, a Dutch national, and several Western governments made repeated appeals to the Iraqi government for information about Ambassador al-Jabiri's whereabouts and welfare. None was ever answered, but some seven months later the director of the Human Rights Division received a handwritten letter purporting to be from the former ambassador. The letter assured that he was alive but said he would not be returning to the United Nations or to the diplomatic service. The letter's authenticity was apparently never proven, nor has it ever been determined precisely what happened to Ambassador al-Jabiri.[80] As may be imagined, Iraqi diplomatic cooperation with the U.N. Human Rights Commission's work on disappearances ceased altogether with Ambassador al-Jabiri's disappearance.[81]

Other Iraqi disappearances have not enjoyed the same degree of international attention as those of Drs. Shahristani and Jaafar and Ambassador al-Jabiri. In 1980, its first year in operation, the Working Group on Enforced or Involuntary Disappearances received reports of over two hundred cases of disappearances in Iraq.[82] Among these were students, academics, engineers, doctors, civil servants, and intellectuals whose disappearance could be linked to such events as the regime's pursuit of members of the Communist party and the Shia al-Dawa organization, or to the regime's expulsion or imprisonment of Iranians and Iraqi citizens of Iranian origin.

Most Iraqis arrested for political or security offenses disappear for a time. When this happens, family members assume that the missing person is in detention. But since inquiries generally go unanswered and may provoke the arrest of other family members or friends, the family often faces an anguished wait that may end with word from or of the prisoner, his release, or notification of his death. Or, the wait may never end. There is no reliable figure for how many people have disappeared in Iraq, but international human rights organizations that have concerned themselves with the issue estimate the numbers to be in the thousands. In the summer of 1989 the Iraqi government announced the creation of a commission to locate persons who disappeared in earlier years, a step evidently meant to be a conciliatory gesture toward the families of the disappeared but which also gives some idea of the dimensions of the problem.

The most massive instance of disappearance known to have occurred in Iraq is that of approximately eight thousand Kurdish Barzani tribesmen taken from camps at Qushtapa and Diyana in Arbil province on July 30, 1983. The Barzani Kurds, under the leadership of Mulla Mustapha Barzani, took part in the Kurdish uprising of 1974–75, which was backed by the Shah of Iran and, secretly, by the United States. Barzani's legendary guerrilla fighters, called Pesh Mergas—or "those who face death"—won from the Iraqi army and held a large area of northeastern Iraq, until Iran cut off their supply of weaponry following an unexpected agreement between Saddam Hussein and the Shah in 1975. With defeat then inevitable, Barzani agreed to lay down his arms on a promise from the Baghdad government that no retaliatory measures would be taken against his followers or their families. The promise was made and promptly broken. Tens of thousands of Barzani and other Kurds were expelled from their homes in the mountainous Barzan and Mergasur districts of northern Iraq and sent to camps in the southern desert. In 1978 most were allowed to return to the Kurdish areas of northern Iraq but not to their native villages. They were obliged to settle in what the Iraqi government called "new towns," in fact little more than refugee camps adjacent to Iraqi military garrisons.

In the second half of July 1983, a little less than three years into the Iran-Iraq War, Iranian forces captured the Iraqi Kurdish border town of Haji Omran and advanced a dozen or so kilometers inside northern Iraq. It was the first time in the war that the Iranians had penetrated Iraqi territory; fighting was heavy and so were Iraqi losses. The Iraqi government charged, no doubt correctly, that Kurdish guerrillas under the leadership of Mulla Mustafa's son Masoud had helped the Iranians in their advance. On July 30, the Iraqi army surrounded camps at Qushtapa and Diyana, well removed from the area of fighting, where Barzani Kurds had been resettled five years earlier. Here is the way one of the Barzani tribesmen who managed to escape described the event:

> On that morning I was awakened by my wife shaking me vigorously. She looked horrified and said: "our camp is encircled by the Iraqi soldiers, we are inside a ring of armoured vehicles." I did not believe what she said but when I looked out of the door I was convinced. . . . Baath soldiers were in full control and ready to open fire. Then from all sides the soldiers came down into the camp, firing their guns. . . . They attacked houses, kicked down doors with their boots. . . . Cries of the women and children of a camp of twenty thousand inhabitants were mixed with the shouts and insults of the Baath soldiers, beating and kicking them. For the inhabitants of our camp it was doomsday.[83]

Males aged twelve to eighty were reportedly rounded up, put in military trucks and driven away; that some of them were serving members of the Iraqi government's own Kurdish militia evidently made no difference. According to several reports, they were first taken to the southern Shia cities of Najaf and Karbala, where the Iraqi regime evidently felt morale-boosting measures were needed, and were paraded as Iranian prisoners of war taken in Iraq's "victory" at Haji Omran. From there they were reportedly sent to camps in the desert near the Jordanian and Saudi borders. Kurdish émigré groups believe that a number of them—perhaps as many as one hundred—were executed, but that many of the others may still be alive in the desert camps. Since July 30, 1983, however, nothing has been heard directly from any of these men. The Barzani women and children were left in the Qushtapa and Diyana camps, but with their men gone they found themselves unprotected and with few means of livelihood.

The Iraqi government has given evasive and misleading answers to inquiries made about this case through the Working Group on Enforced or Involuntary Disappearances. In a note sent the Working Group on October 10, 1988, the Permanent Mission of Iraq in Geneva sought to have dismissed a file of 2,800 names, together with birth dates, of the abducted Barzani Kurds which had been compiled by a Kurdish opposition group. The Iraqi government contended that many Barzani Kurds had collaborated with Iran during the war and during Iran's occupation of parts of northern Iraq and had since fled to Iran. The Iraqi note sought to delay or possibly to invalidate the inquiry by claiming that the lists submitted did not specify the date of disappearance or arrest. This prompted a correction from the Working Group, which pointed out that the communication sent to the Iraqi Mission clearly indicated that all the disappearances had occurred on July 30, 1983.[84]

Although since 1983 no single set of disappearances has been reported on the massive scale of the Barzani Kurds, complaints of disappearances in Iraq continue to be filed with the Working Group. In 1988, a case was filed concerning three Iraqi students in Egypt who have been missing since August 9, 1988, when they were taken to Cairo airport by the Iraqi ambassador and put on a flight to Baghdad accompanied by six Iraqi security officers.[85] In August 1989, a case was filed on behalf of thirty-three Iraqi Assyrian Christian families and individuals—over one hundred persons in all—missing since they returned to Iraq in September 1988 and April 1989 under amnesties declared by the government.[86]

Each year for the past several years, the Working Group on Enforced or Involuntary Disappearances has sought permission from the government in Baghdad to visit Iraq and to conduct an on-site investigation of cases filed with it. The Iraqi government has consistently ignored these requests. In the Working Group's report for 1988, it stated that it believed a visit to Iraq would "make an important contribution to its understanding of outstanding matters . . . within its mandate," and pointed out that the Human Rights Commission's resolution 1988/34 encouraged governments concerned with disappearances "to give serious consideration to inviting the Working Group to visit their country." The Working Group noted, however, that it had received no response to its requests for authorization to visit Iraq.[87]

DEPORTATION

Mass deportations from Iraq have occurred principally in two waves. The first took place in the early 1970s and may have involved as many as one hundred thousand. The second extended throughout the 1980s, and is estimated to have affected from thirty thousand to several hundred thousand.[88] Whatever the precise figure, there is no dispute that a very large number of people were taken from their homes and jobs in Iraq, stripped of their property, and forcibly put across the border. In many cases family members were separated, and those who were not deported were sent to internment camps.

Despite their magnitude, these acts have caused no international outcry. Indeed, they have received hardly any attention at all. Many Western writers on contemporary Iraq make no more than passing mention of them. One reason for the silence seems to be that the victims were mostly Shia Muslims, a group that enjoys little sympathy in much of the West. And all were deported to Iran.

The targets of the deportation of the early 1970s were a community of Shia Faily Kurds living in Iraq near the Iranian border to the east and north of Baghdad, and in Baghdad itself. Also targeted were what the Iraqis called "illegal aliens," Persians who had come for the Shia pilgrimage to Najaf and Karbala—many of them decades earlier—and had stayed. These deportations were carried out in apparent retaliation for Iran's seizure of the islands of Abu Musa and the two Tunbs in the Straits of Hormuz, although the Baath regime's desire to blunt early Shia opposition to its seizure of power probably also played a role. Forty thousand people are said to have been sent across the border in the initial phase in 1971 and 1972, and as many as another sixty thousand may have been deported in the following years.[89]

The second wave of deportations coincided with the rising tension between Iraq and Iran following the overthrow of the Shah and the declaration of the Islamic Republic. The Iraqi government for some time described those deported as Iranian citizens and maintained that only a few hundred had been exiled.[90] Later, in the face of evidence that most in fact held Iraqi citizenship and that their numbers were far greater, the Iraqi government fell back to the designation "Iranian origin," or "Persian Shias," and sought to justify its action by claiming that those expelled were an Iranian "fifth column."[91] Many Western diplomats and at least one American writer on Iraq have accepted unquestioningly both the Iraqi government's assertion that those deported were Iranians and its argument that their expulsion was an inevitable and even necessary measure to assure security in wartime, even though most of the expulsions occurred before the war broke out.[92] The writer, who puts the figure for those expelled at thirty thousand, the lowest of any estimate seriously advanced, reported that when she asked about the expulsion of "Persian Shias" from Iraq, "several Iraqis in Baghdad related that not as much resentment existed toward the government as might have been expected because this group had monopolized certain sectors of the economy."[93]

This comment suggests that there may also have been an economic motive for the deportations. But it confirms that many of those deported were people who, whether they held Iranian or Iraqi citizenship, had lived and worked in Iraq for many years and had played a substantial role in its economy. Their deportation arbitrarily deprived them of their homes, their businesses, and their livelihoods.[94]

The first round of the second wave of deportations began in April 1980, a few days after a terrorist attack attributed to the Shia al-Dawa organization on senior Iraqi government officials at a university ceremony in Baghdad. These deportations also coincided with the execution of Mohammed Baqr al-Sadr, one of Iraq's most influential Shia clergymen and, according to the Iraqi government, the leader of al-Dawa. According to several accounts, at least one hundred prominent Baghdad Shia businessmen, merchants, and factory owners were rounded up, taken to security-police headquarters, stripped of personal documentation, and put across the border into Iran penniless.[95] In the following weeks thousands more were deported, without even a semblance of due process. At times whole families were deported, including children, aged parents, and other relatives. Evidently some Iraqis not of Iranian origin or of the Shia sect were caught up in these deportations, either because they had married into Shia families or because the regime found it a convenient moment to get rid of them.

Here is the account given by one deportee, Dr. Muhamed Hakkak, head of the Electrical Engineering Department at the University of Baghdad until his deportation in July 1980:

I was deported with my family on 3 July [1980] after having been apprehended at the Directorate General of Intelligence since 5 June, during which time my family did not know where I was or what had happened to me. . . . There [at the Directorate General of Intelligence] they put dark glasses on my eyes and chained me to a chair. Someone asked me if I was an Iranian. I said no, I am an Iraqi and carry Iraqi nationality. He said, "Of Iranian origin?" and I said, yes. Then he said . . . "Why didn't you say so; your origin is shit." I was left tied to a chair and blindfolded till 1 July when they untied me, shaved my beard . . . and took me to a place where they brought my family. I was deported two days later.[96]

According to Dr. Abdul Wahab al-Hakim, director of the Commission for the Welfare of Iraqi Refugees, a private voluntary organization in London, the deportations took place in conditions of total deprivation, with people being put across the border with literally nothing more than the clothing on their backs, often forced to walk long distances over difficult terrain, and exposed to inclement weather and bandits. In most cases, young men were reportedly separated from families slated for deportation and were imprisoned or interned, a practice evidently intended to prevent their recruitment into the Iranian army. Deportees have found themselves stateless because Iran does not recognize Iraqi deportees as its citizens and has refused to grant them citizenship. It has set up camps for them and supplied minimal rations but little else. The international community has neglected them almost entirely.

The United Nations High Commissioner for Refugees (UNHCR) has, to date, offered no assistance to this large group of involuntary refugees. Dr. al-Hakim, who for years has sought to interest the UNHCR in their plight, told Middle East Watch that during a visit to Geneva in 1987 he found that the high commissioner had adopted the view—propounded by the Iraqi government—that the deportees were Iranian citizens and thus outside UNHCR jurisdiction. Queried about this by Middle East Watch, the UNHCR acknowledged Iran's insistence that the deportees considered by Iran to be Iraqi nationals be assisted by the international community.[97] But the UNHCR argued that "a majority of the persons were expelled from Iraq during the course of the Iran-Iraq conflict"; therefore, it maintained, they fall under Article 4 of the Fourth Geneva Convention relative to the protection of civilian persons in time of war and thus under the mandate of the International Committee of the Red Cross (ICRC) rather than the UNHCR.[98] The UNHCR concluded its reply to Middle East Watch with the statement that:

> [A]s in the present case where there is an overlapping competence with the ICRC and where UNHCR is satisfied as to the basic protection of the persons concerned, it has taken the position that its involvement would be inappropriate in view of the ongoing complicated and very sensitive negotiations between Iraq and Iran under the auspices of the Secretary-General of the United Nations to settle the underlying differences, including the fact of displaced persons.[99]

The reply by UNHCR can be challenged, first of all, on its assertion that a majority of those deported were expelled during the course of the Iran-Iraq War. The massive deportations of Iraqi Shias began in April 1980, six months before the outbreak of the war. The number of those expelled before the war is not known precisely, but conservative estimates place it at thirty thousand, others at fifty to one hundred thousand. Second, Iraqi deportees are not simply persons who found themselves under Iranian occupation or by chance in Iran at the time of the war (whose case Article 4 of the Fourth Convention is intended to cover); they are persons deliberately put across the border into Iran, that is, involuntary refugees, who should fall under UNHCR jurisdiction. Finally, the argument that UNHCR's involvement would be inappropriate in view of negotiations between Iran and Iraq appears specious because a U.N. agency should not permit the sensibilities of a member state to sacrifice the welfare of such a vulnerable population; because Iraq in any event has refused during these negotiations to take the deportees back or to assume any responsibility for them and thus has no grounds to object to UNHCR involvement; and because the negotiations for a formal peace have been stalled since early 1989, and the stalemate could continue for years.

After having been told of the UNHCR's determination that the Iraqi deportees fell under the mandate of the ICRC, Middle East Watch inquired of both organizations whether they had consulted with one another about helping the deportees. We were assured by spokespersons of each that they had, but details on these consultations were not forthcoming despite our further inquiry. Middle East Watch's inquiries addressed to the ICRC had not been answered when the report issued in February 1990 went to press. An official of the ICRC's New York office told Middle East Watch that so far as he knew the ICRC had not provided relief assistance to the Iraqi deportees in Iran—and Dr. al-Hakim confirmed this—but he believed his organization had helped resettle a few of them outside of Iran.

Although most of the second wave of deportations had taken place by the end of 1981, deportations from Iraq to Iran continued on a smaller scale throughout the 1980s. At present three camps for Iraqi deportees are said to exist in Iran, two in north-central Iran, designated Malawi and Azna, and a third in southern Iran, called Johron. Together, the camps house some fifteen thousand, reportedly in conditions of great deprivation.[100] The deportations have created a large Iraqi Shia community in the Iranian city of Qum, but even those who have found a niche there and in other Iranian cities face an uncertain future.

In the negotiations that followed the cease-fire of August 1988, Iran demanded that Iraq take back two hundred thousand deportees who it said were Iraqi citizens. So far, however, Iraq has refused to take any responsibility for those it deported.

Iraqis whose citizenship documents bear the notation "of Iranian origin" are too numerous to be deported in their entirety; one writer places their number at two million.[101] But while some are loyal servants of the Iraqi regime, many evidently remain vulnerable to summary deportation.[102]

5

THE KURDISH MINORITY

On the maps that show it, the area inhabited by the Kurds of Iraq is a shaded crescent that begins a short distance northeast of Baghdad, runs thickly north along the border with Iran and Turkey, and then tapers off after touching momentarily the border with Syria. On some maps, the crescent's inner rim is heavily shaded, to denote the area where few non-Kurds traditionally lived. A lightly shaded outer strip encompasses the city of Kirkuk and runs along the edge of Mosul; it indicates an area that contains—or once contained—a preponderantly Kurdish population mixed with Arab and Turcoman elements.

These maps—the second in particular—suggest much of the history of the struggle that has raged over almost seven decades between the Kurds of Iraq and the Arab government in Baghdad, a struggle over land, oil wealth, and political and cultural rights. They reveal nothing, however, of the catastrophe visited upon the Kurds of Iraq in recent years: of the ravages caused by the Iraqi government's use of poison gas against Kurdish civilians, by its killing and torture of Kurds, by its deliberate policy of expulsion and forced resettlement, and by its creation of a vast free-fire zone, emptied of population and dotted by the ruins of flattened dwellings, where hundreds or perhaps thousands of Kurdish villages once stood. Today, a realistic map of the Kurdish areas of Iraq would look very different from the smooth schematic ones found in history books or newspapers. Its jagged edges and reduced size would reflect the trauma experienced by Iraq's Kurds.

THE STRUGGLE OVER KURDISH RIGHTS IN IRAQ

The Kurds, it is generally agreed, are the Middle East's fourth largest ethnic and linguistic group, after the Arabs, the Turks, and the Persians. What is not agreed is how numerous they are. Estimates range from eighteen to thirty million. The reason for this imprecision is that the Kurds are divided mainly among four states, Turkey, Iran, Iraq and Syria, none of which cares to know or to make known their precise number.[1] Turkey is generally believed to harbor the largest number of Kurds—ten million or more—but officials rarely concede that Turkey has any Kurdish population at all. It bans the teaching of the Kurdish language and its use in all official settings. Officials in Ankara generally refer to Turkey's Kurdish citizens as "mountain Turks" and have been known to go so far as to argue that the Kurds of Turkey originally spoke Turkish but "forgot" their mother tongue over the centuries.[2] Iran does not go to such extremes, but it has never recognized minority rights for its five or six million Kurds and at times it has prohibited teaching and publication in Kurdish. In both Turkey and Iran, Kurdish nationalism has been harshly suppressed. Syria likewise grants no recognition to its Kurdish population, estimated at three to six hundred thousand. It prohibits both teaching and publishing in the Kurdish language.

There is also no census figure for the Kurds in Iraq, a fact all the more curious because, on paper at least, Iraqi Kurds enjoy a status that awards them both political and cultural autonomy. Iraq's interim constitution of 1970 states: "The people of Iraq is formed of two principal nationalities, the Arab nationality and the Kurdish nationality. This Constitution shall recognize the national rights of the Kurdish People and the legitimate rights of all minorities within the unity of Iraq."[3]

Iraq's "Law for Autonomy in the Area of Kurdistan," promulgated on March 11, 1974, stipulates that "the Kurdish language shall be the official language, besides the Arabic language, in the area" and that "Kurdish shall be the language of education for Kurds."[4] The law of 1974 provides that the autonomous area is to have an elected legislative council and is to constitute an autonomous financial unit with its own special budget. Though accepted by some Iraqi Kurds, the law was promulgated over the objections of the main Kurdish party of the time, the Kurdish Democratic Party (KDP), and its leader, Mulla Mustapha Barzani.

Dispute over the territorial definition of the Kurdish Autonomous Region, as it has come to be known, was among the main reasons for this rejection. The autonomy law was preceded by an agreement of March 11, 1970, between the KDP and the relatively new Baath government which, according to the Kurds, stipulated that the Autonomous Region would include all territories populated by a majority of Kurds and specified that within one year a census would be taken to determine the extent of these territories.[5] Kirkuk province, which contains one of Iraq's richest oil fields, was the main contested area. The Kurds wanted it included in the Autonomous Region and sought allocation to the region's budget of a fixed percentage of the Kirkuk field's oil earnings, a demand the Baghdad government stoutly resisted.

The census was never taken. Kurdish writers charge that instead the Baath government pursued a policy of Arabization of Kurdish lands, not only in Kirkuk province but also to the south in Khanaqin and to the north in the Kurdish districts of Mosul province, in an attempt to diminish the size of the area to be allocated to the Autonomous Region. In September 1971, the Iraqi government deported to Iran several tens of thousands of Faily Kurds, supposedly Iranian citizens or Iraqis of Iranian origin, who had long been established along the border with Iran to the east and north of Baghdad and in the capital itself.[6] In the early months of 1973, the Iraqi army began expelling Kurds from villages in the Kirkuk area and from certain sectors of Iraq's borders with Turkey and Iran.[7] And in 1971 and 1972 Iraqi security services attempted to assassinate Mulla Mustapha Barzani.

Not surprisingly, these actions undermined the Kurdish opposition's confidence in the good faith of the Baath government. Offers of military and financial backing by the Shah of Iran and U.S. Secretary of State Henry Kissinger, through the intermediary of the U.S. Central Intelligence Agency, encouraged Kurdish leaders to resist accommodation with Baghdad. This aside, however, the Kurds felt that the Iraqi government's proposal of March 1974 fell far short of the kind of political and economic autonomy they had been promised in 1970, not to mention in the early 1920s when the Iraqi state was first formed.

From the beginning of the Iraqi state, the Kurds of the former Ottoman Wilayet of Mosul resisted incorporation out of both latent nationalism and fear of domination and exploitation by the new state's Arab majority. In 1919, a year before the mandate state of Iraq was created, a prominent Kurdish tribal leader, Sheikh Mahmoud Barzinji, proclaimed himself king of an independent state and took over the city and area of Suleimanieh. This first experiment in Kurdish statehood soon collapsed. Mahmoud did not have the backing of other Kurdish tribal leaders, and the British easily removed him. A second attempt by Mahmoud, in 1922, also failed. Mahmoud's failure notwithstanding, Kurdish reluctance to be included in the new state was made unmistakably clear in the referendum held in 1921 to approve the appointment of Faisal as king of Iraq. In the Arab provinces, Faisal won overwhelming backing, but in Kirkuk, the majority voted against him, and in the Kurdish heartland city of Suleimanieh, the referendum was boycotted.[8]

Kurdish hopes were raised by the Wilsonian rhetoric of the Versailles peace conference and, more important, by the Treaty of Sèvres, signed on August 10, 1920, between the allied powers and the government of Ottoman Turkey. Section III of the treaty, entitled "Kurdistan," envisaged the establishment of an independent Kurdish state, to be set up first as a League of Nations mandate state.[9] But when Kemal Ataturk repudiated the Treaty of Sèvres, defeated the Greek army in Anatolia, and established himself in uncontested control of Turkey, the allied powers signed a new agreement with his government, the Treaty of Lausanne of July 24, 1923. This document made no mention of Kurdish independence.

Even before the Treaty of Lausanne was signed, the former Ottoman Wilayet of Mosul had become the object of much negotiation and some devious maneuvering between Britain and Turkey. The Turks wanted it placed within their border. The British insisted that it should be a part of Iraq, for London wanted to assure access to the Kirkuk and Mosul oil fields and feared that without these oil resources the mandate state of Iraq would not be economically viable. In December 1922, in an effort to win the Kurds to their side, the British and the new Iraqi government issued a joint statement recognizing "the right of the Kurds who live within the frontiers of Iraq to establish a Government within those frontiers."[10]

The fate of the Kurdish areas was not finally decided until December 1925, when the League of Nations agreed with the recommendation of its Commission of Inquiry that the former Ottoman Wilayet of Mosul should be attached to the state of Iraq. Promises of independence or a formal structure of autonomy were set aside, but the League did put two conditions on its decision, both designed to offer protection to the Kurds of Iraq. One was that the British mandate should continue for another twenty-five years. The other was that: "The desire of the Kurds that the administrators, magistrates and teachers in their country be drawn from their own ranks, and adopt Kurdish as the official language in all their activities, will be taken into account."[11]

The League called on the British government, as the mandate power, to "present before the Council the administrative measures it will take to ensure that the Kurdish populations mentioned in the Commission of Inquiry's report enjoy the type of local administration recommended by the Commission." [12] The Baghdad government responded unenthusiastically by issuing, in 1926, a Local Languages Law. The British Mandate, which the Kurds counted on to protect them from Arab domination, lasted not the twenty-five additional years recommended by the League but less than five. After the Anglo-Iraqi treaty of 1930 granted Iraq independence, the Kurds revolted in protest over the failure of both the British and the Iraqis to carry out the recommendations of 1925.

Kurdish revolts broke out time and again in the decades that followed. The Kurds were in a continuous state of armed rebellion from 1961 to 1970. Inability to curb the Kurdish insurgency contributed heavily to the fall of every Iraqi government during that time—Qassem, the brief first Baath regime of 1963, and Aref. The breakdown of negotiations between Mullah Mustapha Barzani's KDP and the government in Baghdad led to another round of fierce fighting that ended in 1975 when the Shah of Iran and the United States cut off assistance to the Kurds after Saddam Hussein made concessions to the Shah over the Shatt al-Arab waterway.

The Autonomous Region of Kurdistan established by the law of 1974 comprises a territory of 37,062 square kilometers, approximately half the territory that Barzani's KDP and Kurdish writers claim to be home to a Kurdish majority.[13] Although the law stipulated that the Kurdish legislative council was to be elected, seventy-two of the eighty members who convened for the first session, in October 1974, were appointed by the government in Baghdad.[14] At the council's second session, in October 1977, the entire membership was appointed.[15] In the ensuing years, Kurdish autonomy was played up or down according to the Baghdad regime's view of its need for Kurdish support. By 1977, after Baghdad had crushed Barzani's revolt of 1974–75, the Kurdish area was no longer referred to in official Iraqi pronouncements or in the media as "The Autonomous Region of Kurdistan" but simply as "The Autonomous Region." Tens of thousands of Kurds were expelled from their homes and sent to camps in the desert, Barzani's Kurdish Democratic Party was banned, and many of its members were arrested, tortured and executed.

Kurdish sources claimed that up to sixty thousand men were arrested, following the agreement between the Shah and Saddam Hussein in 1975, on suspicion of being members of the KDP or its military arm, and were sent to detention camps in the south of Iraq.[16] Late in 1975, twenty-three Kurds were reportedly arrested on charges of being members of a secret political organization; after trial by a revolutionary court in 1976, three were sentenced to death and others to six years' imprisonment.[17] In 1976 and 1977, over two hundred Kurds were reportedly arrested on suspicion of opposition activities.[18] Over seven-hundred-sixty Kurds were reportedly arrested in 1978.[19] In 1979, the Kurdish Academy, founded in the early 1970s to promote Kurdish culture and books, was disbanded, and compulsory illiteracy-eradication classes in the Kurdish areas were reportedly conducted solely in Arabic.[20]

Attempts to suppress Kurdish cultural identity continued through the first year of the Iran-Iraq War. In 1981, schools in Kirkuk, Khanaqin, Mosul, and Dhok provinces reportedly stopped teaching in Kurdish, and the Kurdish section in the College of Arts in Baghdad was closed. The University of Suleimanieh was moved to Arbil, a city considered more amenable to governmental control, and was renamed Salah al-Din University.[21]

By 1983, with the war going heavily against Iraq, the regime reversed itself and began making conciliatory moves toward the Kurds. The Autonomous Region once again became the Kurdish Autonomous Region. The government entered into negotiations with Jalal Talabani's Patriotic Union of Kurdistan, by then one of the two leading Kurdish opposition groups.[22] In a speech in March 1983, Saddam Hussein declared that talk of Kurdishness did not detract from Iraqi patriotism, provided it did not imply separatism. He urged Kurdish men of letters to write of "the Kurds, their history, literature and culture . . . until our Kurdish people have had their fill."[23] That same month the Kurdish Cultural and Publishing House was reactivated. In April the study of Arabic in Kurdish areas was made compulsory beginning only in the fourth grade, rather than in the first grade as required by the autonomy law of 1974. A festival of Kurdish culture and art was held in the main Kurdish cities in July 1983, at the same time as Iranian and Barzani Kurdish forces were attacking Iraq in the north. The Kurdish branch of the Baath party launched a propaganda campaign stressing that the Baath government had gone further than any other in satisfying Kurdish national rights and that Iraqi Kurds were better off than Kurds elsewhere. The party assured Kurds that the government clearly distinguished between Kurdish "rebels" and the "Kurdish masses."[24] In August 1986 Saddam Hussein for the first time attended the Kurdish Legislative Council's opening session and declared autonomy to be "indispensable for both Iraq and the Kurdish people."[25]

These assurances notwithstanding, autonomy has proven an empty shell for Iraq's Kurds, and the government of the Kurdish Autonomous Region is powerless and the butt of jokes. The Executive is still appointed by the government in Baghdad. Even though since 1980 the Legislative Council has been elected rather than appointed, it has little authority. Its budget is allocated in Baghdad and the central government reviews and can revoke its decisions. Moreover, in 1986 the Baghdad government passed a law requiring that candidates for election to the Council "should have played a well-known role in fulfilling the [Baath Party] principles and aims." [26] And the regime continued to arrest large numbers of Kurds suspected of opposition to its authority, as well as members of their families; it also continued to torture and summarily execute detainees, and to engage in collective punishment in retaliation for attacks on government officials or installations. [27] Kurds who cooperated with the government were rewarded with jobs, money, and favors, but even they were not necessarily immune to these measures. [28]

As the war with Iran drew to a close and the Iraqi government realized it was gaining the upper hand, it no longer felt the need to adopt a conciliatory posture toward Iraqi Kurds. To the horror of the outside world, it attacked Kurdish rebel forces and civilian settlements with poison gas. It also began systematically razing Kurdish towns and villages, expelling their inhabitants, and sending large numbers to "new towns" in the plains of the Kurdish Autonomous Region, and reportedly also to the south of Iraq and to camps in the desert.

CHEMICAL WARFARE AGAINST THE KURDS OF IRAQ

The testimony repeated itself with numbing regularity in over two hundred interviews conducted by U.S. Senate Foreign Relations Committee staffers Peter Galbraith and Christopher Van Hollen, Jr., in September 1988, with Kurdish refugees dispersed in five separate camps in southeastern Turkey. [29] Bechet Naif, a resident of Berkule village, stated that:

At 6:00 a.m. on August 25, eight planes flew over our village. All eight dropped weapons. . . . When they dropped the bombs, a big sound did not come out—just a yellowish color and a kind of garlic smell. The people woke up, and some of them fainted. Those who poured water on themselves lived: those who could not reach the water died. I went into the river. Almost 50 women died. Some died who went to help their families. Seventy-five people died. My brother died. . . .

[And the son of Iskender Ahmad testified that:]

Animals and children died. Blood came from their mouths and a yellow liquid from their mouths and noses. The noise did not sound like regular bombs. They would just drop and make a weak sound and then this cloud. Always expanding: a yellow cloud. Those who escaped managed to go to the water.

These were the accounts given by people from villages in the northernmost corner of Iraq, within a few dozen kilometers of the Turkish border. They were the survivors of chemical-weapons attacks carried out by Iraqi forces from August 25 to 27, 1988, in which thousands of persons are believed to have died. Many of the men were, by their own admission, Barzani Pesh Merga guerrillas. But the great majority of victims were unarmed civilians, including women, children, and the elderly, because, according to the testimony of the refugees, Iraqi warplanes and helicopters for the most part did not drop their bombs on the Pesh Merga camps but on nearby villages.[30] After the attacks, tens of thousands of Iraqi Kurdish villagers set out on foot and with pack animals, across mountainous terrain, for Turkey. Dr. Youssef Hamed, a Kurdish physician who fled with the villagers and attempted to treat them on the way, told a Western journalist who interviewed him in a camp in Turkey:

People died under my hands. It took us one week to walk here. I think in that time I saw 200 people die from the chemical weapons. There are thousands dead, but we could not bring their bodies with us. . . . At Ismasewa, three people were suffering from what I believe was nerve gas. They were hallucinating and could not move in a straight line. They vomited continuously and had severe spasms of the body.[31]

Those who managed to make it to the border by August 27 were able to escape across it. Some of those who came days later still managed to get through, though by then they had to elude Iraqi troops who opened fire in an attempt to block their flight. By early September, according to refugee testimony, most avenues of escape were shut off; Iraqi troops had established a nearly impenetrable cordon along the border with Turkey.[32] Estimates of the number of people who fled in this manner range from sixty to one hundred thousand. Many thousands of other suspected gas victims who lived further from the Turkish border found themselves trapped inside Iraq.

Some six weeks after Galbraith and Van Hollen took testimony from Kurds who fled to Turkey, Gwynne Roberts, a British journalist long familiar with

Kurdish issues, visited Kurdish refugee camps in Iran near the border with Iraq and Turkey. Roberts was the first Western journalist that the Iranians allowed into that area after Iraq's August onslaught against the Kurds. Of his interviews with people in these camps, he later wrote:

> What I found stunning was the consistency of detail provided by the numerous people I talked to. In August and September, I'd been in Angola with Unita which was claiming that nerve gas had been used against their troops by the Cubans/MPLA. I met a group of soldiers who said their injuries . . . were caused by poison gas. Their descriptions of what had happened were so lacking in detail and consistency that I began to have serious doubts about the veracity of their claims. . . . The Kurdish accounts were incredibly graphic. They came from isolated communities all over Iraqi Kurdistan, and despite this were often remarkably similar. It would have been impossible for the people concerned to have invented the stories and then co-ordinated the details with each other. I ran a number of the accounts past a number [of] chemical warfare specialists after I returned home. The point made by several was that many of the victims were illiterate villagers and there was no way they could have known of the effects of these superlethal nerve gases . . . it seemed not a case of whether poison gas had been used but which agents were involved.[33]

Among the testimony Roberts gathered was that of Kurdish Pesh Merga guerrilla fighters who said they had witnessed the massacre by chemical weapons of several thousand Kurdish civilians in the Bassay Gorge, some twenty-five miles south of the Turkish frontier, late in August 1988. Roberts took detailed statements on this incident, which otherwise has passed almost unreported in the Western media. Ramazan Mohammed, aged nineteen, from Mangesh, near De hok, in northern Iraq, told Roberts:

> On August 27th we tried to cross towards Turkey but the main road was blocked so we went to the Bassay Gorge. At dawn on August 28th, the Iraqis started bombing. There were over 5,000 people in the gorge, mostly women and children. The planes were normal war planes. They dropped their bombs and my first sensation was the smell. It was like burnt polythene or plastic or sponge. Then there was yellowish smoke. The women and the children were mostly on the floor of the gorge, in caves or on ledges. The Pesh Merga were guarding the heights. Five or ten minutes after the bombs fell, I noticed people dropping. I was in the

mountain heights and the ones I saw dying were about 100 to 200 meters away from me. They would first cover their eyes with their hands and then shake uncontrollably. They screamed extremely loudly. Soon afterwards they would drop. All their bodies began to tremble violently and then they went still. . . . In the gorge, it smelt like burnt onions. All the trees and all the bushes seemed to have dried out. There must have been some 3,000 bodies there, thousands of animals—all dead. There was a film over their eyes, and horrible slime coming out of their noses and sides of their mouths. The skin was peeling and bubbling up. . . . I didn't dare go closer than thirty meters . . . [but afterwards] I had a cough and breathing was difficult. My eyes were itching and my nose was running.[34]

Of this same encounter Faris Taha, aged seventeen, also from Mangesh, told Roberts:

The first body I saw when I came down from the heights was completely black. I heard the cries of a few survivors which were incomprehensible. . . . Most of the people there were sprawled around dead. There must have been many more than 3,000. They were all huddled together in family groups, and they had died like that. . . . We spent the night in the mountains, and I didn't know how it passed, I have never, never been so scared in all my life. . . . [The next day] I had binoculars and saw thousands of soldiers with gas masks and gloves entering the gorge. From my hiding place, I saw them dragging bodies into piles and then setting fire to them. I saw over a hundred fires.[35]

On September 8, the U.S. State Department publicly condemned Iraq's use of chemical weapons against the Kurds, and Secretary of State George Shultz vigorously rebuked Iraqi Minister of State Saadoun Hammadi, who was in Washington at the time. The State Department's finding that Iraq had used chemical weapons against its northern Kurdish population was based on "intelligence sources"—intercepts of Iraqi military communications which, according to a U.S. official interviewed by Middle East Watch, provided the U.S. clear, albeit unpublishable, evidence of Iraq's transgression. The Iraqi government, however, immediately denied the charge. Hammadi issued the first denial after his meeting with Shultz in Washington on September 8. Foreign Minister Tariq Aziz claimed that the flight of Iraqi Kurds to Turkey reflected nothing more than their realization that the rebel cause was doomed once the cease-fire between Iraq and Iran had come into effect.[36] President Saddam Hussein expanded on this thesis in a press interview on September 9:

> A group of collaborators was used by Iran along with its occupation army to harm Iraq's military efforts in northern Iraq. When the Iranian army was expelled from the borders, naturally this group of collaborators lost any military might that would make it capable of confronting our Army. Therefore, it collapsed. And when our army advanced toward the Turkish borders . . . [the collaborators] used threats to intimidate some villages, telling them the Iraqi army would allegedly think of them as outlaws. Some of these village residents escaped or entered Turkish territory under the duress of the saboteurs.[37]

Iraq's denial yielded a similar response by Turkish officials. Turkish doctors who at first had told U.S. diplomats that the Kurdish refugees showed clear signs of exposure to chemical agents changed their story or fell silent after the Foreign Ministry in Ankara issued a statement denying that Turkey had evidence that Iraq had used poison gas.[38] "We have thoroughly looked into it," a Foreign Ministry official said in Ankara on September 10. "There were . . . a few deaths of people who showed some signs of sickness and there were autopsies on the bodies. The examination of them did not show any evidence of chemical weapons being used."[39] From then on, Turkish doctors described the illness of Kurdish refugees as stemming from intestinal infections, malaria, hepatitis and other diseases common in the region. "These aren't from chemicals," Dr. Sinan Seyfioglu, a Turkish physician at one of the refugee camps, told a *New York Times* correspondent on examining the blisters across the face of a three-year-old Kurdish boy. "This sort of thing is not unusual. It comes from malnutrition and improper medical care and poor cleanliness."[40] Speaking of the Iraqi Kurdish refugees, an official of the Turkish Red Crescent, Dr. Mustafa Yildez, told Western reporters, "I don't see in this population signs of chemical weapons."[41] Other Turkish doctors made similar statements to Western reporters.

Two facts deserve note with regard to the Turkish endorsement of the Iraqi position. First, since as early as the 1930s Turkey and Iraq frequently have cooperated in suppressing Kurdish dissent. In 1982 the two governments signed an agreement authorizing Turkey to send its armed forces into Iraq in pursuit of rebel Turkish Kurds or in joint operations with the Iraqi army against rebel Iraqi Kurds.[42] On several occasions during the Iran-Iraq War, Turkish forces crossed the Iraqi border to strike at Kurdish insurgents. Second, Turkey and Iraq are major trading partners. Turkey gets most of its oil from Iraq, and during the Iran-Iraq War it is believed to have extended some two billion dollars in still unreimbursed credits to Iraq, according to a U.S. official interviewed by Middle East Watch.

Moreover, Turkish doctors evidently made their exculpatory diagnoses solely on the basis of visual physical examinations. No effort was made, in the early days when conclusive results could still have been obtained, to run the kind of blood and urine tests that might have resolved whether the Kurdish refugees had been exposed to chemical weapons. Despite the transparency of Turkish motives, others promptly picked up the theme that the victims' allegations were unsubstantiated and unpersuasive. Although Galbraith and Van Hollen had been struck by the consistency and the detail of the Kurdish refugees accounts (as had Roberts in Iran), a few Western correspondents announced that the Kurds' stories were "confusing and lacking in detail." [43]

In the United States, journalist Milton Viorst argued that the case against Iraq was "shaky." He acknowledged that "Iraq probably used gas—of some kind—in air attacks on rebel positions." But, Viorst suggested, the symptoms seen by journalists at the camps in Turkey "could have been produced by a powerful tear gas, a conventional weapon in today's warfare." [44]

Hardly anyone in the West was ready to join Viorst in ignoring both the numerous testimonies of the victims and the mass of circumstantial evidence. The Senate Foreign Relations Committee staff report concluded that "overwhelming evidence exists that Iraq used chemical weapons on Kurdish civilians in a major offensive in northern Iraq that began August 25, 1988." [45] A team of American doctors sent by Physicians for Human Rights conducted extensive examinations in refugee camps in Turkey from October 7 to 16, 1988, and concluded categorically that "Iraqi aircraft attacked Kurdish villages in northern Iraq with bombs containing lethal poison gas on August 25, 1988." [46] In November 1988, Gwynne Roberts clandestinely entered Kurdish areas of Iraq, under escort of Pesh Merga guerrillas, and brought out samples of the soil where an Iraqi chemical bomb had fallen. A British laboratory and scientists who examined the samples concluded that they contained chemicals "consistent with mustard gas." [47]

In mid-September, at the urging of the United States, the Soviet Union and eleven other countries, United Nations Secretary General Perez de Cuellar asked permission of Iraq and Turkey to send a team of U.N. experts to investigate charges that Iraq had used poison gas against the Kurds. Here was a chance, at a date sufficiently early to be persuasive, for Iraq to make its case before an impartial international body, and for Turkey to dispel doubts about the sincerity of its denials. Instead, with a timing that suggested coordination, both governments promptly rejected the secretary general's request. A Turkish government spokesman called the proposed investigation "unnecessary and unwelcome." [48] Iraq dismissed it out of hand. Speaking to Western journalists at a press conference in Baghdad, Iraqi Defense Minister Adnan Khairallah commented that "the Kurds are Iraqis and it is an internal issue." There was, Khairallah said, "no justification" for the United Nations or any international party to infringe upon Iraq's sovereignty by independently investigating conditions in Kurdish areas of Iraq. "I want," the defense minister added in a remark that conveyed more than was perhaps intended, "to deal with a certain segment of my population in the way I want." [49]

Instead of the United Nations investigation, the Iraqi government invited a group of twenty-four Western journalists. To no one's surprise, their carefully supervised helicopter tour of Kurdish areas in late September 1988 brought to light no physical evidence of chemical-weapons use. But through an evident glitch in Iraqi planning, the journalists were given a glimpse of what the world suspected. *Washington Post* correspondent Patrick Tyler reported: "In a bizarre moment on Saturday, dozens of reporters at the military air base at Mosul passed an Iraqi Army truck whose driver and passengers were wearing gas masks." [50] Taken to the Turkish border on the promise that they would witness the return of a thousand Kurds from Turkey, the reporters waited for an hour before Iraqi officials announced that "technical difficulties" had prevented the Kurds from crossing. [51] The journalists found that they were not allowed to speak freely with Kurdish villagers, television crews were required to turn their videotapes over to Iraqi authorities, and a *New York Times* dispatch was first censored and then barred from transmission. [52]

The gas attacks on the Kurds in August 1988 were not the first case of Iraq's use of chemical weapons. Iraq was first reported to have used chemical agents in its war with Iran in 1983. In March 1984 both the United States and the United Nations publicly denounced Iraq's use of poison gas. Despite international protest, Iraq made increasingly frequent use of chemical weapons as the war proceeded. According to a U.S. official interviewed by Middle East Watch, U.S. military sources determined that chemical weapons during these years became a regular part of the Iraqi army's arsenal and its military doctrine. Iran has claimed that fifty thousand people, many of them civilians, were killed or wounded by Iraqi chemical weapons between 1983 and 1988.[53] But almost until the end of the war, Foreign Minister Tariq Aziz, Defense Minister Khairallah, and other Iraqi government spokesmen consistently and often vehemently denied all charges that their government was employing poison gas. In March 1984, when the United States first announced that evidence in its possession showed Iraqi use of chemical weapons, Khairallah accused the United States of "political hypocrisy" and declared that Iraq did not need chemical weapons. "The conventional weapons we own are capable of achieving what you have seen on the battlefield. . . . No chemical weapons were used."[54] As late as January 1988, Tariq Aziz denied to American congressmen visiting Baghdad that Iraq had ever used poison gas.[55]

In employing chemical weapons in its war with Iran, Iraq placed itself in direct violation of its obligations under the Geneva Protocol of 1925, which bans "the use in war of asphyxiating, poisonous or other gases." The Protocol, however, does not ban the production and stockpiling of chemical weapons. Since 1974, Iraq has been engaged in a major effort to build plants to manufacture chemical agents. Since 1985, it has been producing substantial quantities of chemical agents, including mustard gas and two different types of nerve gas.[56] Today it is said to have the largest and possibly the most sophisticated chemical-weapons program in the Third World.[57] It reportedly has stepped up its production of chemical weapons since the end of the war with Iran[58] and is believed by one analyst to be trying to develop a biological-warfare capability.[59]

Iraq's defenders argue that it did not literally violate the Geneva Protocol of 1925 when it used chemical weapons against its Kurdish population. The language of the Protocol simply bans the use of chemical weapons "in war." Based on the intent of the drafters, some jurists take the view that the Protocol applies only to international armed conflict, since that was the concern at the time of the states that drew it up. The Arab League ambassador to the United Nations, Clovis Maksoud, sought to use this legal loophole in Iraq's defense when the United States, Britain, and others condemned Iraq's use of chemical weapons against the Kurds in August and September 1988. The Arab League envoy pointed out that the 1925 Protocol prohibited the use of chemical warfare only between states and did not say anything about the use of such weapons within sovereign borders. He objected strongly to the United Nations being called upon "to investigate a matter within the prerogatives of sovereignty."[60] On the other hand, a leading expert on international humanitarian law consulted by Middle East Watch expressed the view that the prohibition on poison-gas attacks had assumed the status of customary international law, and thus would be prohibited in all circumstances, despite the limited scope of the Protocol.[61]

Whether or not the Protocol applies to Iraq's gas attacks on its Kurds, these attacks clearly violate Iraq's other international obligations. Article 6 of the International Covenant on Civil and Political Rights prohibits the arbitrary deprivation of life, regardless of the means used. And even if the gas use were said to have occurred in the course of a civil conflict, common Article 3 of the Geneva Conventions of 1949 would prohibit killing of noncombatants without proper trial.

The gas attacks of August 1988 were also not the first against the Kurds.[62] According to Kurdish sources, on April 15 and 16, 1987, the Iraqi government launched poison-gas attacks on villages in Suleimanieh and Arbil provinces, in zones controlled by Kurdish rebels. The attacks reportedly left more than 300 dead and wounded. According to one uncorroborated report, when some 380 survivors of the April 16 attacks went to hospitals in Suleimanieh, Kirkuk, and Arbil, Iraqi authorities first issued orders that they not be treated unless they affirmed in writing and on Iraqi television that Iran was responsible for the attacks. The victims were then allegedly rounded up and sent to the Arbil military camp where they were executed and buried.[63]

The gas attacks of April 1987, and other such attacks on Kurdish villages that reportedly occurred in May, June, and September of the same year, attracted little attention because few of the victims escaped to bear witness. Only when pictorial evidence of the horror of chemical warfare against defenseless civilians became available, following poison-gas attacks on the Iraqi Kurdish town of Halabja near the Iranian border on March 16 and 17, 1988, did the world take serious notice. Western television crews filmed ghastly scenes of bodies strewn along Halabja's streets, families locked in an embrace of death, lifeless children, doll-like with blackened mouths, eyes, and nails, and the upended carcasses of domestic animals.

Halabja had been seized some days earlier by Iranian forces aided by Kurdish Pesh Merga guerrillas. When word first spread of massive deaths from poison gas, there was speculation that both Iraq and Iran may have been responsible; the civilian Kurdish population may have been caught, some said, in chemical-weapons attacks launched by both sides. But according to the testimony of survivors, the chemical weapons employed in Halabja were dropped from airplanes well after the town had been captured by Iranian and Kurdish forces and after fighting in the immediate area had ceased. Although Halabja lies within Iraq's borders, it was Iran, not Iraq, that raised an outcry after it was bombed. Iran promptly filed a vigorous protest with the United Nations, requested a U.N. investigation, and invited the international media and humanitarian organizations to Halabja to view the bodies of those killed by chemical weapons and to interview survivors. The specialist sent by U.N. Secretary General Perez de Cuellar, Dr. Manuel Dominguez, a colonel in the Spanish army's medical service, visited Iran from March 28 to 31, and examined sixty-six patients in hospitals. He concluded his report with these words: "The clinical examinations I conducted in the Islamic Republic of Iran showed that the patients had been exposed to chemical weapons. A large number of them were civilians."[64] Colonel Dominguez then visited Iraq and examined chemical-weapons victims being treated at al-Rasheed hospital in Baghdad. Whereas the patients he examined in Iran were for the most part civilians who were listed as having been gassed at Halabja on dates between March 16 and 18, the patients in Iraq were soldiers whose date of injury was given as March 31 at a "military position near Halabja" or a "town near Halabja."[65] Iraq produced no victims or evidence to sustain allegations that the gas attack at Halabja in mid-March was the work of Iran.

During a visit to Iran in April, an independent expert, Professor A. Heyndrickx, head of the Department of Toxicology of the University of Ghent, Belgium, took blood, urine, and hair specimens from survivors of the Halabja attacks. In a report published on April 27, he concluded that in each case "there is no scientific doubt that the patient is intoxicated by . . . chemical warfare agents."

Middle East Watch was told by a U.S. official that, according to U.S. intelligence sources, on March 16, the first day of the chemical bombing, Halabja was swollen to a population of some 70,000 by refugees from Kurdish villages to the west that had been destroyed by the Iraqi army. Although some estimates put the number killed as low as 600, most placed it in the thousands. A French correspondent later put it at 3,500.[66] An official of the International Committee of the Red Cross who visited Halabja privately estimates that some 5,000 Kurds and a much smaller number of Iranian soldiers were killed in the gas attack and the Iraqi shelling of the town.[67] Other estimates exceed 6,000.[68]

Despite the international outcry, Iraq stepped up its use of chemical weapons in the spring and summer of 1988, both in its war against Iran and in attacks on Iraqi Kurds. On May 9 and again on August 26, 1988, the United Nations Security Council condemned the use of chemical weapons in the Iran-Iraq War and called on both sides to refrain from future use of such weapons, pursuant to their obligations under the Geneva Protocol of 1925. Nonetheless, Kurdish opposition sources claimed that there were chemical-weapons attacks on Kurdish villages in Iraq on March 22, 24, 24, and 27, April 14 and 27, May 5 and 15, July 20, 30, and 31, August 3 and 8, from August 25 through much of the month of September, and on October 11 and 14. The attacks on July 30 and 31 reportedly took place along the Turkish and Syrian borders. They were a precursor to the attacks in late August that provoked the flight of villagers to Turkey.

Many saw Iraq's resort to chemical weapons against the Kurds as President Saddam Hussein's way of exacting revenge for their having sided with Iran during the war. No doubt there is an element of truth in this, for the use of chemical weapons was apparently militarily unnecessary. Even before the cease-fire with Iran came into effect, Iraq began massing an army of some 60,000 in Kurdish areas of Iraq, a force that international experts judged more than enough to crush the Kurdish rebellion by conventional means.

But revenge may not have been the only consideration. As Iraqi Defense Minister Khairallah pointed out in his press conference on September 15, 1988, poison gas was not a "logical" weapon to use in mountainous terrain, where it could "pollute an area in the vicinity of our troops."[69] But poison gas was an extraordinarily effective weapon to use to create panic and thus swiftly to empty the Kurdish mountains of their population, an aim the Iraqi government had been pursuing for some time. Once the war with Iran came to a close, the government moved expeditiously to carry this program to its conclusion. Villages and towns where Kurds had lived for centuries were razed, and hundreds of thousands were moved to new settlements in the low-land areas of the Kurdish Autonomous Region and, according to Kurdish sources, to the south of Iraq and to camps in the desert or on the desert's edge.

FORCED RESETTLEMENT:
THE DEPOPULATION OF KURDISH AREAS

The Iraqi government began its most recent program of forced resettlement of Kurds in 1985. The program assumed substantial dimensions beginning in 1987. The precise number of those displaced cannot be known because of the secrecy with which the Iraqi government has shrouded the operation, but it is generally estimated at least 500,000 and maybe higher.[70] This massive uprooting, which threatens to undermine if not destroy Kurdish ethnic identity, and in which several thousand Assyrian Christian villagers and other minorities have been caught as well, has taken place with little more than a murmur of public protest by Western governments and without condemnation or criticism of any sort by the United Nations or its associated agencies.

Iraq's current displacement of its Kurdish population is not its first effort to dilute their presence in traditional areas. In 1963, following Qassem's overthrow, the first Baath government offered incentives to Iraqi Arabs to settle on the fringe of Kurdish areas. This grew in later years into a more ambitious effort at "Arabization" of certain areas inhabited mainly or wholly by Kurds. After the quelling of the Kurdish uprising of 1974–75, the second Baath government expelled large numbers of former Kurdish guerrilla fighters, along with their families, to the desert and to southern Iraq; some Kurds and Assyrians who may not have been involved at all in the fighting were also forced from their homes. Some of those who were expelled were allowed to return to northern Iraq within a few years but were barred from returning to their villages. The luckier among them were permitted to resettle in the major Kurdish cities, Suleimanieh, Arbil, and Dehok. Many were sent to "new towns" in the plains areas of the Kurdish Autonomous Region—at the time little more than detention camps in the vicinity of army posts. The Iraqi government justified this program by claiming that in the new towns it would be possible to provide the Kurds "the requirements of progress and civilization," that is, health care, electricity, running water, and other amenities.[71] These settlements, which according to Kurdish opposition groups offered few if any of the advertised services and little or no opportunity for employment, were constructed with development funds allocated, amid much publicity, to the Kurdish Autonomous area.[72] Parallel to this the government began a program of forcibly resettling Kurdish villagers from border areas. From June 1978 to April 1979, Kurdish opposition groups reported, the government forcibly resettled some 250,000 Kurds from villages in the Turkish and Iranian border areas to new towns.[73] Demonstrations reportedly broke out in Kurdish areas of Iraq late in 1978 and early in 1979 in protest over harsh living conditions in the new towns.

The expulsions were put on hold during the early years of the Iran-Iraq War as the Iraqi government negotiated with Kurdish rebel leader Jalal Talabani.

These negotiations broke down in 1985 and Talabani joined forces with Masoud Barzani, son of the late Mulla Mustapha, in open insurrection against Baghdad. The insurgents seized large areas adjacent to the Turkish and Iranian borders, and many Kurds who had earlier been expelled from these areas moved back and reestablished their homes. As Iraqi forces reconquered these areas, in the closing phase of the war, systematic expulsions began again and extended to Kurdish villages that had remained in government hands—and in some cases loyal to the government—during the war.

The Iraqi government has acknowledged uprooting a segment of the Kurdish population, but it claims to have done so for their security and benefit. "We are just moving people out of range of artillery fire, we are building them new houses in the Kurdish areas," Iraq's ambassador to the United Kingdom, Mohammed Sadiq al-Mashat, told a British newspaper in June 1989.[74] According to another Iraqi official, the relocation program is part of a government project to develop the Kurdish area after "long years of backwardness."[75]

A fuller (and no doubt more carefully coordinated) explanation was offered in official statements issued by Iraq's ambassadors in Washington, London, and other Western capitals on June 26, 1989. "The Iraqi government decided to create a depopulated strip of land, no more than 30 kilometers wide inside our territory and all along the 1200 km boundary lines with both Iran and Turkey," the ambassadors announced. This, they said, was done because of "the bitter experience suffered by our towns and villages along the border with Iran throughout the eight years of the Iranian aggression, and in view of the barbaric bombardment and destruction to which the population of these areas were subjected." The statement added that "this measure is not limited to the Autonomous Region of Kurdistan in the North but is extended to the provinces of the midlands and the South. The provinces of Basrah, Missan, Wasit, Dyala, Sulaimaniyah, Arbil and Dhawk have all benefited from this protective measure."[76] The ambassadors' statement assured that the Iraqi government had made payments of between 5,000 and 10,000 Iraqi dinars to families being resettled,[77] and that "each and every family has been allocated a piece of land which they could live on and cultivate in peace and safety."[78] To this, Iraq's ambassador in Washington, Dr. Abdul Amir al-Anbari, has added the oral assurance that all Kurds moved from their homes were being resettled in the Kurdish Autonomous Region of Iraq.[79]

In this as in other matters, the Iraqi government has yet to allow systematic independent verification of its claims. But the eyewitness testimony that has emerged from visits in recent years to the Kurdish areas of Iraq by Western officials and journalists flatly contradicts the Iraqi government's claim that the depopulation effort has affected only a strip of land parallel to the Turkish and Iranian borders and that its sole or even main concern is the welfare of the population. According to a U.S. official interviewed by Middle East Watch, a Western official who visited the Kurdish areas of Iraq in September 1987 saw Kurdish villages leveled all along the road leading from Baghdad to Suleimanieh and also along the road from Suleimanieh to Kirkuk, far from the 30 kilometer border zone. Throughout the Kurdish areas, this official said, villages were being razed. A U.S. Senate Foreign Relations Committee staff member who visited Iraq that same month reported:

> [T]he Iraqi army has, over the past few months, been dynamiting the evacuated Kurdish villages. In at least one case the Army requisitioned earth-moving equipment from a foreign engineering firm so as to eliminate any traces of previous habitation. With hundreds of villages leveled, the Kurdish countryside has an eery, deserted quality to it. Fruit trees, graveyards, and cemeteries stand as reminders of the absent people and livestock. The Iraqi Army conducts itself in Kurdistan as if it were a foreign occupying army. Iraqi soldiers were observed harassing Kurds at checkpoints, demanding papers capriciously and bullying local youths.[80]

As for the new towns, the Senate staff member wrote:

> These sprawling settlements, which bear names like "Victory City," are designed, in the words of one Iraqi Army Officer, "to control better the Ali Baba," (a derogatory term used by Iraqi Arabs to describe the Kurds).[81]

American journalists who were invited to visit Iraq a year later, in September 1988, as part of the government's effort to refute charges that it had used poison gas, were able to witness the further effects of this program. *New York Times* correspondent Clyde Haberman reported:

> From a low-flying helicopter, the systematic leveling of Kurdish Iraq becomes evident. Scores of villages have been reduced to patches of stone and cinderblock rubble across a 120 mile stretch of the country's far north, from the Iranian border in the east to this battered hamlet [Bamarni] close to Turkey. Where Kurdish villages still stand, they seem

deserted. No activity can be seen. Roads run past these places, but they carry no vehicles.[82]

And *Washington Post* correspondent Patrick E. Tyler wrote:

This part of Kurdistan has been burning. All that remains is the scorched earth, bombed-out villages and the rotting harvest abandoned by more than 5,000 Kurdish refugees. . . . What is clear from a helicopter survey of the region today is that dozens of Kurdish villages have been razed, attacked or dismantled in a sweeping campaign by the Baghdad government to remake the face of Kurdistan, ancestral home of at least 2 million Kurds.[83]

With the departure of the Western journalists at the end of September 1988, the Iraqi government once more drew a veil of secrecy over its expulsion of the Kurds. The veil was not pierced again until April 1989, when the story of the forced evacuation of Qalat Diza reached the Western press.[84] Qalat Diza was a small Kurdish city north of Suleimanieh and some ten kilometers from the Iranian border. Evidently because of its size—at least 50,000 inhabitants or more—it was not affected by the earlier rounds of expulsions. On March 29, 1989, however, according to the international press, the inhabitants of Qalat Diza and a number of other towns and villages in its vicinity were instructed to prepare to depart. Iraqi authorities told them that they would be allowed to take only personal belongings they could carry, and that they should leave their homes in good order; the latter command raised fears that the government intended to bring Arabs from southern Iraq, or Egyptian or Yemeni Arabs, to settle the city.

The population refused to comply. It sent a delegation to Baghdad to appeal to President Saddam Hussein for exemption from the expulsion program. The leader of this delegation, Mulla Muhammad Delgaii, disappeared in Baghdad and was later reported to have been imprisoned.[85] Possibly owing to the publicity that the evacuation order momentarily achieved, it was temporarily suspended. But in late May 1989 the Iraqi army moved to take up positions around the city, and in June Kurdish opposition sources reported that the entire population, some 16,000 families, had been expelled from Qalat Diza.[86] The city itself, according to an Iraqi Information Ministry spokesperson, has been razed.[87]

The Iraqi government claims that "the people of Qalat Diza and its villages were granted the right to choose for themselves the place in which they

wanted to live anywhere in the autonomous provinces of Arbil and Sulaima-
niyh."[88] Kurdish opposition groups say the people of Qalat Diza were asked
to choose one of three relocation camps in Arbil and Suleimanieh provinces
but that these may have been only way stations to internment in desert camps
or dispersal in southern Iraq.

Estimates of the number of Kurdish towns and villages destroyed by the
government vary widely, and the Iraqi government is not known to have issued an official figure. Iraqi opposition spokesmen say that at least 4,000 of
approximately 5,000 Kurdish towns and villages—some 80 to 85 percent—have been destroyed since the Baath regime first instituted its program
of forced relocation in the mid-1970s. The figure cited by U.S. State Department officials is much lower, approximately 11,200, but these officials are
uncertain how it was arrived at or whether it was meant to be comprehensive.[89] A noted expert on Kurdish issues estimates that approximately 75 percent of the villages and towns in the Kurdish area of Iraq have been destroyed
and their inhabitants forcibly relocated.[90]

Most of those forcibly relocated have been from the Kurdish highlands
which today are virtually empty. The "new towns" to which many were sent
are in the Kurdish lowlands. Twenty-two are reported to have been built, a
dozen of them in Suleimanieh province. A French reporter invited to observe
the elections to the Legislative Assembly of the Kurdish Autonomous Region
in September 1989 described the new towns as "located near the cities, like
Suleimanieh, in easily accessible areas along the main roads, in the middle of
vast plains with thin vegetation where the army is very much present (a third
of the Iraqi army is stationed in Kurdistan)."[91] A British correspondent who
visited Kurdish areas of Iraq in August 1989 was allowed to tour one of the
towns to which survivors of the poison-gas attack of March 1988 had been
relocated. He reported:

> "The new Halabja" is 12 miles away from the old town. . . . It is a
> featureless expanse of single-room, half-built houses buried in piles of
> sand and cement, and surrounded by small military posts. At its entrance
> is a portrait of Saddam Hussein, President of Iraq. An official reminds
> us that the town's name is in fact Saddamite Halabja, in honor of the man
> who "has done so much for the Kurds". . . . The 50,000 residents of
> old Halabja who have been moved to the new town were given a piece
> of land and a subsidy to build a house. Regardless of official assertions
> that nobody wants to leave, many do. In the half-finished gateway to his

bungalow, Hoshmen Mustafa Fattah says that he would return to the old town "tomorrow if I could—it is my home." His wife, tending a sunflower plant, nods her head vigorously.[92]

This and other recent Western journalistic accounts tend to corroborate the Iraqi government's claim that those relocated have been given a plot of land in one of the new towns and monetary compensation, although the compensation is less than the 5,000 to 10,000 dinars reported in the ambassadorial statement of June 26, 1989. (Western correspondents put the compensation at 11,500 dinars for rural people and somewhat larger sums for urban dwellers.) The relocated Kurds nonetheless face major problems in their new homes—problems of adjustment from life in the mountains to life in the hot, dry plains and, above all, problems of employment. Few have enough land to survive by farming, the only occupation most know. Some reportedly have found jobs in light industry in Suleimanieh, Arbil, and Dehok, but unemployment is rife. To escape starvation, according to a State Department official interviewed by Middle East Watch, many have been obliged to join the Iraqi government's Kurdish militia, the Fursan, which offers small monthly payments, or to have become informers for the police and security agencies. Kurdish exile groups claim that people in the new towns suffer from a general sense of disorientation and a widespread feeling of demoralization and bitterness.

But where have the rest of the approximately 500,000 internally displaced Kurds gone? Many are said to have squeezed in with relatives in the three remaining cities, Suleimanieh, Arbil, and Dehok, swelling the population. Some reportedly have been sent to live in urban areas in the Arab south of Iraq. Others still—the less fortunate, those marked by the regime for retribution—have reportedly been sent to detention camps in the desert near the Saudi and Jordanian borders. Little is known for sure about these camps. Kurdish opposition spokesmen cite the names of three camps: Ar Ar, Nughrat Salman, and Rutba. Kurdish opposition spokesmen say that persons detained in these camps suffer from the great extremes of desert heat and cold, from lack of food and water, and from terrible psychological and cultural deprivation.

The depopulated areas have been made into free-fire zones in which the Iraqi army follows a policy of shoot to kill, according to an expert on Iraqi and Kurdish affairs interviewed by Middle East Watch who requested anonymity. Kurdish sources claim that since the spring of 1989 the Iraqi regime has also taken measures to restrict the Kurdish population of the cities in Kurdish areas, that Kurds have been prohibited from buying or building new homes there or expanding existing ones, and that Kurds who were not residents in these cities prior to 1975 have been obliged to register with the authorities, a step that has sparked fears that they may be expelled to the new towns or the desert internment camps. Owing to the secrecy maintained by the Iraqi regime, these reports, and others that allege measures to restrict the teaching of Kurdish, could not be verified.

The motives behind the Kurdish resettlement program are quite different from the benevolent one of protecting people professed by Iraqi government spokesmen. By uprooting the population along the borders with Iran, Turkey, and the northeast corner of Syria, the Iraqi government has, for one thing, surrounded and neutralized Iraqi Kurds, cut them off from contact with Kurds in neighboring countries and prevented them from ever again obtaining military or other assistance across the Iranian, Turkish, or Syrian borders. By extending the expulsion program to rural Kurdish areas of Iraq outside the 30 kilometer security zone, the government evidently seeks both to punish rebel villages and to deprive the rebels of their population base. The Barzani and Talabani Pesh Merga guerrillas were able to operate successfully in the Kurdish mountain areas because they enjoyed the sympathy of the population and drew logistical support and recruits from it. One of the calculations behind the forced relocation program was that the Kurdish rebellion could not survive the extinction of its civilian-population base in the mountains. The newly constructed urban agglomerations to which the Kurds have been forcibly sent were chosen by the authorities for convenience of control, with no consideration for the preference, health, welfare, and employment opportunities of the Kurdish population. The consequences for the future of the Kurdish minority in Iraq are bound to be immense.

ETHNIC IDENTITY AND THE QUESTION OF GENOCIDE

What does this massive upheaval mean for Kurdish identity and cultural survival in Iraq? Even before the mass expulsions of the late 1980s, the Kurds' way of life had ceased to be exclusively rural. For some time, Iraqi Kurds have been migrating to urban areas and making their way in business and the professions. But Kurdish civilization and society is still strongly rooted in rural ways and traditions, and even many urban Kurds look to their village and tribal origins. Life in Kurdish mountain villages was never as idyllic as it is sometimes portrayed, but it was the bedrock of Kurdish ethnic identity. The sudden, brutal uprooting of large numbers of Iraqi Kurds is bound to be deeply disturbing to the entire society. By all accounts, the main Kurdish cities continue, for the moment at least, to function much as before. But can cities survive without a rural base? And with the rural underpinnings of Kurdish life and culture in Iraq now smashed, can the Kurds themselves survive there as a recognizable ethnic group?

Some have charged that Iraq's actions against its Kurdish population amount to genocide, a crime under international law. Genocide has been called "the ultimate crime and the gravest violation of human rights."[93] The prohibition against genocide was codified in the "Convention on the Prevention and Punishment of the Crime of Genocide" of December 9, 1948. Article II of the 1948 Convention defines genocide as:

[A]ny of the following acts committed with intent to destroy, in whole or in part, a national, ethnic, racial or religious group, as such:

(a) Killing members of the group;
(b) Causing serious bodily or mental harm to members of the group;
(c) Deliberately inflicting on the group conditions of life calculated to bring about its physical destruction in whole or in part;
(d) Imposing measures intended to prevent births within the group;
(e) Forcibly transferring children of the group to another group.

Though exact numbers cannot be known, many thousands of Iraqi Kurds have been executed, tortured, killed, or irremediably sickened by chemical weapons. It might be argued that, terrible as it surely is, the toll inflicted upon the Kurds by the Iraqi government is of a lesser order than that suffered by other groups generally agreed to have been victims of attempted genocide. The Iraqi government has not tried to eliminate the Kurds through an organized program of slaughter. The scale of killing (paragraph [a] of Article II of the Convention) has nonetheless been substantial. This, together with the expulsion of several hundred thousand Kurds from their homes, the deliberate destruction of their villages and towns, the disappearance of thousands or perhaps tens of thousands of Kurds inside desert camps, their exile to other parts of Iraq, and their forced resettlement in new towns in harsh and controlled conditions, violate several well-recognized provisions of international human rights and humanitarian law and raise a question of genocide under the terms of paragraphs (b) and (c) of Article II of the Genocide Convention. Forced relocation has unquestionably caused serious bodily and mental harm to a large Kurdish population, and appears to be part of a deliberate attempt to inflict on the Kurds of Iraq conditions of life that are calculated over time to bring about the disappearance of Kurds as an identifiable ethnic group in Iraq.

The definition of genocide under the Convention of 1948 turns on the matter of intent, and intent, even in the clearest of circumstances, is difficult to prove. Insofar as the practical effect of Iraqi actions is concerned, the findings of this study accord generally with those of the Senate Foreign Relations Committee staff report of September 21, 1988: if not genocide under the meaning of the Convention, the policy pursued by Iraq toward its Kurdish citizens has unmistakable characteristics of genocide.[94]

Several of the headings of the Nuremberg Tribunal's charge of "crimes against humanity" could apply as well to Iraq's actions against the Kurds and against other elements of its population. The tribunal defined these as "murder, extermination, enslavement, deportation, and other inhumane acts committed against any civilian population . . . or persecutions on political, racial, or religious grounds . . . whether or not in violation of domestic law of the country where perpetrated."

There is, of course, no effective enforcement mechanism either for the Genocide Convention or, since the Nuremberg International Military Tribunal adjourned in October 1946, for crimes against humanity. Were there such a mechanism, Middle East Watch believes that there would be sufficient evidence to compel a careful review of Iraq's case and of the responsibilities of its leaders.

THE MARDIN POISONINGS

In June 1989 the international media reported that some 2,000 Iraqi Kurds at a refugee camp near the city of Mardin, in southeastern Turkey just above the Syrian border, had fallen ill and were claiming to have been poisoned by Iraqi agents. These people were among the approximately 60,000 Kurds who had fled the Iraqi chemical-weapons attacks in late August 1988. They had spent a difficult winter in temporary shelter with little in the way of medical, sanitary, or social services. Turkish authorities immediately labeled the mass illness food poisoning, which they attributed to "unhygienic bread." In the United States and Western Europe, Kurdish charges of deliberate poisoning by Iraq were generally dismissed as the paranoid imaginings of a panic-stricken refugee population, or as an attempt by Kurdish opposition groups falsely to incriminate the Iraqi government.[95]

Accompanied by Dr. John Foran, head of the London-based International Medical Relief, British journalist Gwynne Roberts flew to Turkey to investigate.[96] On arrival at Mardin, Roberts and Foran found the town "thick with police and army." Unable to enter the Kurdish refugee camp, they met by prearrangement with a Kurdish contact who told them that Turkish journalists had attempted to interview poison victims at the local hospital but had been prevented from doing so by the security police; the Turkish police had then turned the sick out of the hospital and forced them to return to the camp. From this Kurd, Roberts and Foran obtained bread and samples of blood and urine taken from patients five days after they fell ill. They were also given a videotape taken secretly in the camp that showed the victims twitching in agony. On the tape a young Kurd testified that his mother had complained of dizziness and fatigue just minutes after eating dinner and that "by the next morning she couldn't talk, then she began to find difficulty in opening her eyes and breathing." Kurds at the camp reportedly complained that Iraqi agents walked about openly in Mardin and had tried to intimidate them and assassinate their leaders. They thought the poison might be thallium.[97]

Tests run on the bread samples at London's National Poisons Unit at New Cross Hospital and at the Robens Institute in Guildford showed no trace of thallium. Further tests at Southampton University and at the Ministry of Agriculture and Fisheries came up negative both for organic toxins and heavy-metals poisons. However, Swedish scientists suggested that the symptoms were typical of organophosphorus poisoning. Analysis of the blood samples done at the British National Poisons Unit revealed "unmistakable signs that blood enzymes had been attacked by a supertoxic organophosphate—a compound grouping associated with pesticides and chemical warfare agents."[98] The British scientist who analyzed the blood samples, Ivan House, told Roberts that "there can be little doubt that these people were affected by a potent nerve agent." Another British scientist, Dr. Alistair Hay, lecturer in chemical pathology at Leeds University, said "the chances of it being an accident are very remote. . . . This was not the sort of chemical you would find on the shelf of a garden shop." [99]

Victims at Mardin camp reportedly complained of convulsions, paralysis, difficulty in breathing, partial blindness, and acute abdominal pain. There were no deaths, but pregnant women were said to have miscarried. The evidence turned up by Roberts's investigation is inconclusive. But it strongly suggests that the mass illness that broke out among Kurdish refugees at the Mardin camp on June 8, 1989, may have been the result of deliberate poisoning by agents of the Iraqi government using a chemical-warfare compound.

6

THE TREATMENT OF IRANIAN
PRISONERS OF WAR

Although two years have passed since the cease-fire of August 1988, neither Iraq nor Iran has returned more than a small number of the prisoners of war. According to the ICRC, Iraq is believed to hold between thirty and forty thousand Iranians, and Iran some seventy thousand Iraqis.

In continuing to hold these prisoners, both Iraq and Iran have placed themselves in clear and flagrant violation of international law. The Third Geneva Convention, to which both Iraq and Iran are parties, stipulates in Article 118 that prisoners of war shall be released and repatriated without delay after the cessation of active hostilities. The government of Iraq claims that it is prepared to repatriate Iranian prisoners unconditionally.[1] In fact, Iraq conditions its readiness to do so on Iran's willingness to release Iraqi prisoners. (Iran has at various times demanded that Iraq withdraw from all Iranian territory before it would agree to the repatriation of Iraqi prisoners of war.) Since the convention admits of no conditionality whatsoever, not even that of reciprocity, Iraq as well as Iran stands in violation of its international legal obligations. The fact that prisoners of war continue to be held so long after the termination of hostilities makes the violation more egregious.

Iraq's record on the treatment of Iranian prisoners of war is a mixed one. (The matter of Iran's treatment of Iraqi prisoners falls outside the scope of this study.) On the positive side, Iraq has allowed the ICRC to register a substantial number of its Iranian prisoners of war and to make regular visits to those it has registered. It has permitted the United Nations Secretary General to send two missions, in January 1985 and July 1988, to investigate the conditions in which Iranian prisoners are being held. And in 1985 it allowed a French private voluntary organization, Terre des Hommes, to open a school for Iranian children who were prisoners of war, although it closed the school four years later.

In its collaboration with the ICRC, however, Iraq has fallen short of its obligations under the Third Geneva Convention. In July 1988 the government of Iraq ordered a halt to ICRC registration of Iranian prisoners. Iraq claimed it was acting in reprisal against Iran, which it contended had denied the ICRC access to a large number of Iraqi prisoners. Until registration was ordered halted, the ICRC had registered just over eighteen thousand Iranian prisoners held by Iraq. In the two years since that date there have been no further registrations. Here again the government of Iraq stands in violation of its international legal commitments, for the Third Geneva Convention admits of no conditionality in the matter of ICRC access to prisoners, not even conditionality based on reciprocity.

The mission dispatched by the United Nations Secretary General in January 1985 to investigate conditions in Iraqi prisoner-of-war camps reported substantial violations of the standards of treatment required under the Third Convention.[2] The mission found considerable delays in submitting the names of prisoners to the ICRC. It reported that large numbers of Iranian prisoners were being held in covert camps—specifically the Abu Ghoraib prison where torture and political killings have been frequently reported to be practiced on the Iraqi political and criminal offenders incarcerated there. The mission was told that the Iraqi authorities had moved Iranian prisoners from their camps in order to prevent their meeting with the ICRC and even with the mission itself. (Iraq acknowledged moving prisoners from time to time but claimed this was done for the purpose of interrogation only, and that prisoners were always returned to their camps afterwards.) And the U.N. mission heard serious allegations of brutality:

In almost all camps visited we met POWs who had had their hearing impaired, including several who had lost their hearing in one ear and even some who had become totally deaf as a result of blows on their head or ears. We were also told that some POWs had lost their sight or had had it seriously impaired as a result of beatings. We noticed scars, bruises, broken teeth and other bodily marks which appeared to be consistent with the stories told us by the prisoners. Other frequent forms of punishment mentioned to us included confinement in punishment cells for periods of up to a month, and individual and collective deprivation of food.[3]

The United Nations mission also reported substandard camp conditions, inadequate medical care, and a good deal of suffering among the prisoners.[4] Prisoners claimed that other prisoners had died or become seriously disabled because of a lack of medical attention.

The mission dispatched by the United Nations Secretary General in July 1988 reported that improvements had taken place since the visit of the previous mission in 1985.[5] Conditions in camps had improved. Problems of ill treatment of prisoners and violence against them had not entirely been solved but progress has been made. The mission found that Iraqi prison camps were being regularly visited by the ICRC and its recommendations were generally being complied with.[6] The mission visited four POW camps, each chosen independently. In two of the camps visited, those holding newly captured prisoners, the mission found reasonably good facilities and services. In a third camp it found evidence of overcrowding, complaints about living conditions, and allegations of guard violence, though on a lesser scale than during the 1985 visit.[7] At the fourth camp, the mission found that prisoners who complained during the visit of abusive treatment were subsequently threatened and may even have been assaulted by the guards and the camp commander.[8]

The U.N. missions of 1985 and 1988 each reported that Iraq held substantial numbers of Iranian civilians in internment. These fell into two categories:

1. Persons Iraq claimed were refugees seeking protection from political oppression in Iran. This is by far the largest group, numbering, according to the January 1988 report, some 55,000 and comprising people of Iranian-Kurdish and Iranian-Arab origin. The mission visited a camp for people of Iranian-Kurdish extraction, which it found to be surrounded by barbed wire; it described conditions there as "rather grim."[9]
2. Civilians held in prisoner-of-war camps and treated as POWs, said in the 1985 report to number more than 1,500.

The justification given by Iraqi authorities for holding this second category of persons was that they had been met with arms in hand. The U.N. mission of July 1988 found, however, that "there is reason to believe that many of these prisoners were genuine civilians, many of whom had been deported from areas under Iraqi occupation."[10] The most prominent Iranian civilian held in this manner by Iraq is former minister of oil Mohammed Javad Tondguyan. Although clearly a civilian and captured in the oil-producing city of Abadan on November 9, 1980, Mr. Tondguyan continues to be detained.

Iraq also continues to hold seriously wounded or ill prisoners, both adults and children. Iran and Iraq each repatriated small numbers of seriously wounded or ill prisoners in November 1988 but the program was terminated before completion when each side accused the other of failing to return all those agreed upon. Iraq repatriated another 255 wounded or ill Iranian prisoners in January 1989 but is believed still to hold more. The Third Geneva Convention requires immediate repatriation of all wounded or sick prisoners, without waiting for termination of hostilities and with no condition of reciprocity.

In the course of the war Iraq took prisoner many hundreds, perhaps thousands, of Iranian children aged twelve and older who had been drafted and sent to the front lines by the government of Iran. So far as is known, none of these children have been repatriated, and in the years since their capture the older among them have grown to adulthood and are now detained and treated as regular adult prisoners. In January 1985, Terre des Hommes opened its school at the Ramadi 7 prisoner-of-war camp. The school had a difficult history. The first director was expelled in December 1985, and the organization reported incidents of guards beating child prisoners for minor offenses. The school was used as a showplace to which foreign journalists were brought, and Terre des Hommes protested this exploitation for propaganda purposes.[11] The government of Iraq closed the school down in February 1989, alleging that the number of young prisoners was by then insufficient to justify its continuing existence. Terre des Hommes claimed that the action was politically motivated and that twenty-three prisoners aged eighteen or under remained in the Ramadi 7 camp.[12]

7

THE UNITED STATES AND IRAQ

State Department officials insist that human rights are a consideration in the formulation of U.S. policy toward Iraq. "We want as good relations with Iraq as are sustainable," one official said, "and human rights are a factor in what is sustainable." [1] The stated intention is laudable, but U.S. actions have fallen far short. Except in the matter of Iraq's use of chemical weapons—and even then with little consistency—the Reagan and Bush administrations have paid scant attention to human rights in their dealings with Iraq. Both have put the nurturing of newly friendly relations with President Saddam Hussein's government well ahead of addressing the violent and repressive nature of his regime.

THE TURNABOUT IN RELATIONS BETWEEN THE UNITED STATES AND IRAQ

For more than two decades following the overthrow of the Hashemite monarchy in 1958, U.S.–Iraqi relations were marked by suspicion and hostility. In 1959 Iraq left the U.S.-backed Baghdad pact and aligned itself with the Soviet Union. In June 1967, it severed its diplomatic ties with the United States in protest of Israel's occupation of Palestinian lands following its victory in the Six Day War, as did Egypt, Syria, and a number of other Arab states. Unlike Egypt, however, Iraq rejected a U.S. proposal for the establishment of interests sections in each capital. [2] Accordingly, for the next five years the two governments maintained no official contact whatsoever. In 1972, out of a desire to reestablish trade ties with the United States, the Iraqi government changed its position, and interests sections headed by midlevel diplomats were opened in Baghdad and Washington. Iraqi officials made clear, however, that this step would not herald a change in political relations, noting that their government still held the United States responsible for Israel's occupation of Arab lands and would not consider restoring diplomatic ties with the United States until the United States persuaded Israel to withdraw from the lands it occupied in 1967 and to take back Palestinian refugees. The U.S. Interests Section in Baghdad was allowed access to only a restricted number of midlevel officials at the Foreign Ministry and only on matters that Iraq defined as of direct bilateral interest.

The Iraqi government turned aside overtures made by the Carter administration for renewal of diplomatic ties. It opposed President Carter's Middle East peace efforts and, when they resulted in the Camp David accords, denounced them, severed diplomatic relations with Egypt, and led the drive to expel Egypt from the Arab League. As late as February 1980, President Saddam Hussein declared: "We have no diplomatic relations with the Americans—we consider them to be the enemies of the Arab nation and enemies of Iraq, and we have been acting on this basis for the past twelve years. . . . So long as the United States is occupying our land through the Zionist entity, we will continue to look upon it as an enemy of the Arabs."[3]

By 1982, the Iraqi government was beginning to rethink its stand toward the United States. Iraq had suffered serious reverses in its war with Iran and was still smarting from the Soviet decision at the beginning of the war to stop supplying heavy arms to it. In 1982 and 1983, Iraq put out feelers to Washington.

These found ready acceptance, for the United States too was beginning to reassess its view of Iraq. Human rights obviously were not a major part of that reassessment for, even putting aside Iraq's use of chemical weapons, the war brought an intensification of repression at home, including executions, disappearances, torture, and widespread arrests of perceived opponents. Instead, geopolitical considerations were the moving force in Washington. Many in the Reagan administration had begun to look upon the Hussein regime as the main bulwark against Iranian domination of the entire Near East and its vital oil reserves. U.S. policymakers reportedly concluded that an Iranian defeat of Iraq would not only put Iraq's vast oil resources under the control of the regime of Ayatollah Khomeini but would also threaten the oil-rich, pro-Western governments of Saudi Arabia and the Persian Gulf emirates.

This reassessment of Iraq by the United States coincided with and was encouraged by steps taken by Baghdad during the early years of the war to draw closer to the "moderate" Arab states of Egypt, Jordan, Saudi Arabia, and the Persian Gulf emirates—and to the United States' NATO ally Turkey. In August 1982 President Saddam Hussein even softened his stand on Israel. In a meeting with Congressman Stephen Solarz of the United States, he declared that "a secure state is necessary for both Israel and the Palestinians."[4] U.S. officials did not expect Baghdad to assist their Middle East peace efforts, but they came increasingly to feel that Iraq would no longer be likely to obstruct these efforts.

In 1984 formal diplomatic relations were restored and the following year ambassadors were accredited in Washington and Baghdad. The United States also weighed in heavily on Iraq's side in the war with Iran, a process that had begun even before diplomatic relations were restored. In the ensuing years, the United States led a campaign to cut off the flow of Western arms to Iran (while at the same time secretly providing sophisticated weaponry to Tehran), reportedly gave Iraq access to intelligence on Iranian military dispositions, spearheaded the drive for a Security Council resolution ordering a halt to the fighting, and provided naval escort for tankers of Iraq's neighbor and ally, Kuwait. The naval-escort operation led to clashes between U.S. and Iranian forces in the Gulf in 1987 and 1988.

TRADE AND ARMS

With the warming of relations, the United States began providing Iraq billions of dollars in credit guarantees for the purchase of agricultural and industrial products. The war with Iran caused Iraq to borrow on a massive scale, which in turn caused Iraq's credit rating to drop. In their concern over Iraq's mounting foreign debt and their increasing uncertainty whether the government in Baghdad would be able to withstand Iran's onslaught, Western banks, including those in the United States, became reluctant to loan money to Iraq. In 1983, the U.S. government stepped in to ease Iraq's burden by providing credits through the U.S. Commodity Credit Corporation's (CCC) credit-guarantee program for the purchase of U.S. agricultural products. Through 1988, Iraq acquired more than $2.8 billion in U.S. agricultural products under the CCC credit-guarantee program. In 1989, the year following the Reagan administration's public rebuke of Iraq for using chemical weapons against its Kurdish population, the Bush administration doubled the CCC program for Iraq, raising credits to a level exceeding $1 billion dollars in 1989. In addition to credit guarantees, the CCC program has also included some interest-free loans and some direct sales at prices subsidized by the U.S. government.[5]

In 1984, the U.S. Export-Import Bank began extending short-term loan guarantees of up to one year to Iraq for the purchase of goods manufactured in the United States. In the 1970s, the Export-Import Bank had been authorized to do business with Iraq, but that authority was terminated in 1979, when the U.S. State Department placed Iraq on the list of countries found to be sponsoring terrorism. In 1983, the State Department removed Iraq from this list after Iraq expelled the Abu Nidal Black June terrorist group.[6] By then, however, the Export-Import Bank shared many of the commercial banks' reservations about lending to Iraq. It resumed operations only at the insistence of the Reagan administration, under what one bank official described to Middle East Watch as "political pressure." In 1984 and 1985, the bank made some $35 million in short-term loan guarantees to Iraq but discontinued the program after Iraqi borrowers failed to meet repayment schedules. In 1987, again as a result of administration pressure, the bank resumed short-term lending guarantees to Iraq. In July of that year, a $200 million revolving fund was set up, out of which approximately $235 million in short-term credit guarantees was made available in the next two years for the purchase of U.S. products, at U.S. government-subsidized interest rates. This time as well, the bank found the Iraqi government delinquent in meeting some of its repayment schedules.

The Export-Import Bank's reluctance to make heavy credit commitments to Iraq drew criticism from the Reagan administration and the business community. Professional banking standards, not human rights, were the reason for the reluctance to expand its lending to Iraq. The Iraqi government refuses to release economic and financial data, and it has a spotty loan-repayment record. A State Department economist commented:

> Iraq's trade people want great relations with the U.S. . . . . That's because they need official credit; it's better than commercial credit because it's easier to reschedule. . . . The U.S. suppliers and contractors see [the Export-Import Bank] as an obstacle. Ask any of them if they would put themselves on the line for eventual payments from the Iraqis. They sure wouldn't do it, but they have no problem asking their government to do so.[7]

The United States has long maintained an embargo on the sale of military equipment to Iraq. The ban appears to have been strictly enforced on weaponry itself. Around the periphery, however, there have been at least occasional breaches. In 1985, Washington approved the sale of forty-five Bell helicopters to Iraq, a $200 million deal. The sale was conditioned on Iraqi government assurances that the helicopters would be used only for civilian transport. In September 1988, it was learned that some, if not all, of the aircraft had been transferred to the Iraqi military. A group of U.S. reporters who visited the Kurdish areas of Iraq that month at Baghdad's invitation were flown in one of these helicopters. The craft was painted in military colors and piloted by an Iraqi military officer who, reporters noted, was clearly familiar with the terrain. The reporters saw another six to ten U.S.-made Bell helicopters parked on the aprons of military airfields in northern Iraq.[8]

U.S. companies are also said to have been involved in helping Iraq's military industry develop a missile production capability. Hewlett-Packard and other U.S. companies are reported to have supplied equipment to the Saad 16 complex near Mosul, which has been described as "relevant to missile production."[9] Scientific Atlanta, a maker of antennas, and Wiltron, which manufactures sophisticated engineering equipment, are also reported to have supplied equipment that has facilitated Iraq's ballistic missile program. In May 1989, the U.S. Customs Service seized a shipment of vacuum pumps bound for Iraq. The pumps, manufactured by CVC Products, Inc., of Rochester, New York, were believed to have "possible nuclear application."[10]

THE STATE DEPARTMENT'S HUMAN RIGHTS REPORT

The State Department's annual country reports on human rights practices in Iraq have, with minor exceptions, been candid and accurate since 1979, when reporting on Iraq began. The report on 1988, drafted by the Reagan administration and issued in February 1989, stated forthrightly: "Iraq's abysmal human rights record remained unacceptable in 1988." It pointed out that political killing, torture, and disappearance were routinely practiced by the Iraqi government.

With regard to Iraq's actions against its Kurdish minority, the report noted "the grave human rights violations when the Iraqi armed forces moved to crush a longstanding Kurdish rebellion. . . . The campaign was marked by the use of chemical weapons against guerrillas and civilians alike." The report also pointed out that in 1988 the Iraqi government intensified its destruction of Kurdish and Assyrian villages in northern Iraq and its relocation of their inhabitants.

The report failed, however, to provide significant information on the conditions in which the estimated 500,000 displaced Kurds now live. Nor did it discuss the serious ramifications of their expulsion from their native homes and their resettlement in unfamiliar surroundings where few opportunities for regular employment exist. The country report also failed to mention the proliferation of Iraqi laws that call for the death penalty, many of them for crimes clearly of a political nature or of insufficient gravity to warrant capital punishment under generally accepted international standards.

In a few instances, the report resorted to understatement. For example, political and individual rights were described only as "sharply limited" when in fact they are nonexistent. The same misleading term was used to describe the right of peaceful assembly and association. In the section on workers rights, the report merely noted that "no strikes have been reported for almost 20 years," rather than acknowledging that strikes are prohibited.

MATCHING WORDS WITH ACTION

Despite the abuses described in the country reports on Iraq, the U.S. government has fallen disappointingly short when it comes to matching words with action. It is almost as though, having issued its annual report on Iraq, the administration considers its duty done and the matter dropped for the rest of the year, unless particularly egregious new violations take place.

During interviews with Middle East Watch, State Department officials, both in the Bureau of Near Eastern and South Asian Affairs, which has direct operational responsibility for relations with Iraq, and in the Bureau of Human Rights and Humanitarian Affairs, showed themselves keenly aware of the abusive and repressive nature of the Iraqi regime. One senior official of the State Department described the Iraqi government as "possibly the worst violator of human rights anywhere in the world today." Yet, when asked, these same officials expressed considerable reluctance to press Iraq on human rights issues. Some argued that the Iraqi government is "uniquely impervious" to criticism or pressure on human rights grounds. Others argued that despite the substantial political support and trade credits extended by the United States in recent years, there is little or nothing Washington can do that would make a difference.

As a result, the United States has failed to act, or has acted only inadequately, on a series of issues:

Despite the forthright statement in the most recent country report that Iraq's record is "abysmal" and "unacceptable," the Bush administration did not raise with Iraqi authorities the report's findings of murder, extralegal detention, torture, and disappearance of political opponents and government critics, according to State Department sources.

Although the U.S. government has repeatedly denounced forced internal relocation in Nicaragua and Ethiopia, for example, there has been no public expression of concern over the Iraqi government's relocation of at least 500,000 Kurds and Assyrians, although State Department sources said that the U.S. ambassador in Baghdad privately discussed this issue with Iraqi officials during 1988 and 1989.

So far as it has been possible to determine, no formal consideration was given to human rights criteria in the U.S. government's decision to provide CCC credit guarantees and Export-Import Bank short-term credits to Iraq. Section 112 of the Agricultural Trade Development and Assistance Act provides that human rights practices should be taken into account in decisions on financing the sale of agricultural commodities. Evidently this provision of the law was ignored.[11]

The State Department chose simply to ignore and to excuse Iraq's *prima facie* breach of faith in transferring U.S.-supplied helicopters to military control, despite U.S. law barring military sales to "any country the government of which engages in a consistent pattern of gross violations of internationally recognized human rights."[12] State Department officials took the position that the transfer was not a violation of the conditions of sale because there was no evidence that the craft had been used in combat.[13] When the issue became public, Congressman Howard Berman pointed out that the painting of the helicopters in military colors clearly suggested military use.[14] The State Department, however, did not file a protest with the Iraqi government over the transfer or seek to investigate it, according to U.S. officials interviewed by Middle East Watch.

The State Department made no move to reinstate Iraq on the list of countries sponsoring terrorism (it was removed from that list in 1983) despite the fact that the PLO official who masterminded the hijacking of the Italian cruise liner *Achille Lauro* in 1985, Mohammed Abu Abbas, maintained a residence in Baghdad and spent a substantial part of his time there in the years before and after the hijacking. U.S. citizen Leon Klinghoffer was killed by the PLO terrorist team during the course of the hijacking. The department and the U.S. Embassy in Baghdad made repeated representations to Iraq asking that Abu Abbas be expelled or handed over to Italian authorities, who have a warrant out for his arrest. The Iraqi government made obfuscatory responses to the U.S. demarches and continued to harbor Abu Abbas. Had Iraq been returned to the list of states sponsoring terrorism it would automatically have become ineligible for CCC and Export-Import Bank credits.

THE SECRETARY OF STATE TALKS TOUGH—AND RETREATS

Iraq's use of poison gas against its Kurdish citizens in late August and early September 1988 drew a vigorous protest from Secretary of State George Shultz. According to U.S. officials interviewed by Middle East Watch, during a visit to Washington on September 8 by Iraqi Minister of State Saadoun Hammadi, a member of President Saddam Hussein's inner circle, Shultz made known publicly, in extraordinarily candid and undiplomatic terms, his and the Reagan administration's dismay over Iraq's action. At the State Department's noon press briefing on September 8, 1988, the spokesman announced that the United States condemned Iraq's use of chemical weapons and that Secretary Shultz would be raising the issue with Hammadi during their meeting that afternoon. Later that day, the department's press office issued the following blunt statement:

The Secretary today conveyed to Iraqi Minister of State Hammadi our view that Iraq's use of chemical weapons in its military campaign against Iraqi Kurds is unjustifiable and abhorrent. The Secretary stressed to Dr. Hammadi that we attach great importance to the future development of our relationship with Iraq, but that we do not intend to pursue this course if illegal Iraqi use of chemical weapons and other human rights abuses continue. The Secretary asked that the Iraqi government weigh this factor fully in its decision-making. With our friends and allies in the world, we will be exploring ways in which we can influence Iraq to end these practices, which are unacceptable to the civilized world.

According to some official U.S. sources interviewed by Middle East Watch, the vigor of the secretary of state's reaction stemmed in large part from his own personal revulsion over Iraq's use of poison gas. Many in the State Department felt that he had acted impulsively and considered the September 8 press statement issued after Shultz's meeting with Hammadi too harsh. The tough trade-sanctions bill passed by the Senate on September 9 alarmed state department officials who, in the words of one U.S. official interviewed by Middle East Watch, then proceeded to "walk the Secretary back" to a more conciliatory position. Pressed by the Bureau of Near Eastern and South Asian Affairs, and evidently without countervailing pressure from the Bureau of Human Rights and Humanitarian Affairs, Secretary Shultz approved a recommendation that the administration oppose congressionally mandated sanctions. He acceded to the urgings of his Middle East professionals not to punish Iraq for what it had done but rather to try for "deterrence" by holding out the threat of policy (not legislative) sanctions should Iraq use chemical weapons again.

The United States took no other concrete step to manifest displeasure. The administration did not recall the newly arrived U.S. ambassador in Baghdad,[15] and U.S.-government trade credits and guarantees were not eliminated or reduced, but instead were doubled the following year. As columnist Jim Hoagland wrote in the *Washington Post* on October 12, "after publicly convicting Iraq of using poison gas, the State Department [was] now saying the Iraqis should pay no price for their crime."

Nonetheless, Secretary Shultz's protest to Hammadi, the press statement of September 8, 1988, and the momentary threat of congressionally mandated sanctions succeeded in capturing the attention of the Iraqi government. On September 17, 1988, Foreign Minister Tariq Aziz, speaking in Baghdad, declared that Iraq respects and abides by all provisions of international law, including the Geneva Protocol of 1925 prohibiting the use of poison gas. Three days later, the State Department called this "a positive step" and added: "We take this statement to mean that Iraq foreswears the use of chemical weapons in internal as well as international conflicts." Assistant Secretary of State for Near Eastern and South Asian Affairs Richard Murphy told Congress on October 13 that Tariq Aziz had personally confirmed to Shultz that Tariq

Aziz's statement of September 17 meant that Iraq intended to renounce the use of chemical weapons against domestic and foreign enemies.[16]

In late September 1988, however, the administration voiced no protest when the Iraqi government expelled a senior officer of the U.S. embassy in Baghdad, Haywood Rankin, chief of the embassy's political section. Rankin is not known to have violated any rules of diplomatic or personal conduct. His transgression appears to have been that of asking questions about Iraq's use of poison gas during a trip through Kurdish areas in the aftermath of the August and September attacks. There was also speculation that Rankin's expulsion was the Iraqi government's way of retaliating for Shultz's public denunciation of its use of chemical weapons. The State Department responded by expelling an Iraqi diplomat stationed in Washington, but it did not announce the expulsion or link it to the chemical-weapons issue.

In the closing months of 1989, the State Department began an effort to show greater concern over the human rights situation in Iraq. In September, Assistant Secretary of State for Human Rights and Humanitarian Affairs Richard Schifter met in Washington with the legal adviser to the Iraqi Foreign Ministry for a discussion of human rights. Although information available to Middle East Watch suggests that the outcome of this meeting was far from satisfactory, it has been billed by State Department officials as a "broadening" of the U.S. "human rights dialogue" with Iraq. At the end of November, Schifter met with Iraq's ambassador to the United Nations for further talks on human rights issues. But in a major address on U.S. policy in the Middle East delivered on October 27, 1989, Assistant Secretary of State for Near Eastern and South Asian Affairs John Kelly ignored entirely the matter of Iraq's human rights violations. He stated simply: "Iraq is an important state with great potential. We want to deepen and broaden our relationship." [17]

CONGRESS AND THE SANCTIONS BILL

Members of both houses of Congress joined with Secretary Shultz in denouncing Iraq's use of poison gas against its Kurdish citizens. Unlike the administration, Congress at first seemed prepared to match words with action. On September 9, the Senate passed a bill proposed by the chairman of the Senate Foreign Relations Committee, Claiborne Pell, and supported by Senator Jesse Helms, calling for tough sanctions against Iraq. The bill forbade the sale of military equipment of any kind, prohibited the granting of credits or credit guarantees, barred the sale or transfer of any item subject to export controls by any agency of the U.S. government, and banned the import into the United States of Iraqi petroleum products. The Senate bill would have put an end to both CCC credits and Export-Import Bank loans to Iraq.

The Senate bill died in the House Ways and Means Committee, which professed objections to it on procedural grounds. Although an overwhelming majority of House members expressed support for sanctions, there was considerable opposition to cutting off CCC credits, particularly among U.S. farm interests. On September 27, the House passed a bill which its supporters called "a measured response" to Iraq's use of chemical weapons. The bill barred the sale to Iraq of arms, goods, or technology on the control list of the Export Administration Act and chemicals determined to be of use in the production of chemical weapons. U.S. government credits and credit guarantees and Iraqi petroleum imports were put on a list of optional sanctions that the president could invoke against Iraq should it continue to use chemical weapons or fail to provide "reliable assurances" that it would not use such weapons in the future.

This watered-down bill drew objections from exporters who stood to be barred from selling Iraq items on the Export Administration Control List. Congressman William Frenzel criticized the bill on grounds that it would "unduly punish U.S. business by basically turning over their sales to foreign competitors." [18] U.S. companies, at the urging of the U.S.–Iraq Business Forum, quietly lobbied against it.

Nonetheless, the House bill passed by a huge bipartisan majority of 388 to 16, reflecting deep congressional and public concern that the United States take some—albeit limited—steps to punish Iraq. On October 11, the Senate approved by a no less impressive majority—87 to 0—a revised bill almost identical to the one passed by the House on September 27. Although the stage seemed set for the enactment of sanctions legislation, the measure met a somewhat inexplicable death in the jungle of last-minute parliamentary maneuvering before Congress adjourned for the November elections.

Despite these setbacks, Senate Foreign Relations Committee Chairman Pell and other legislators have continued to press the case for sanctions. In June 1989 Senator Pell presented an amendment to the Foreign Assistance Act that would require the president to make a determination whether Iraq consistently commits gross abuses of human rights. Aware that such a determination, if honestly made, would have to be in the affirmative, the Bush administration opposed the amendment, arguing once again, according to congressional sources, that Iraq is "impervious to leverage." The State Department's Iraqi desk officer, Philip Remler, lamented that "Congress is not very protective of our relationship with Iraq." [19]

At the end of September 1989, Senator Daniel Inouye put a rider on the Foreign Assistance Appropriations Act that barred the bank from further dealings with Iraq. The Inouye amendment, itself later amended to allow a presidential override of the ban, became law in November. At year's end, the fate of the Pell amendment was still uncertain.

U.S. ACTIONS IN INTERNATIONAL FORA

Having escaped penalty in its relations with the United States, the Iraqi government managed also to escape censure in international fora. Its success was due at least in part to slack U.S. efforts to secure international condemnation.

The Paris Conference on Chemical Weapons of January 1989

Iraq's use of poison gas against the Kurds prompted President Reagan in a speech before the U.N. General Assembly in September 1988 to call for an international conference on chemical weapons. French President Mitterrand, who went so far as to propose an international embargo on weapons sales to any country using poison gas, immediately picked up the Reagan proposal, and it was agreed that France would host the conference. It quickly became apparent, however, that neither the United States nor France intended to use the conference to condemn or even censure Iraq. Instead, the French decided and the United States agreed that the conference would aim for an international consensus in principle against chemical warfare and for the strengthening of the Geneva Protocol of 1925 barring the use of chemical weapons.

The conference was held in Paris at the beginning of January 1989. Its closing declaration, issued on January 11, reaffirmed "the importance and continuing validity" of the 1925 Protocol and stated that the participating states were "determined to prevent any recourse to chemical weapons by completely eliminating them." Iraq was not mentioned by name but did receive an indirect slap on the wrist, in a passage that recalled the conferees' "serious concern at recent violations as established and condemned by the competent organs of the United Nations."[20] This, however, was a reference only to Iraq's and Iran's use of poison gas in their war against each other, not to Iraq's chemical attacks on its own Kurds. The United Nations never had the opportunity to "establish and condemn" the attacks on the Kurds because both Iraq and Turkey rejected the secretary general's request to send a U.N. investigative team.[21]

The final irony is that the Kurds were barred altogether from the Paris conference because one of the ground rules laid down by the French specified that only states could attend. The French reportedly told Iraqi Kurdish leaders that, because of a threatened boycott by Arab states, the Kurds would not be permitted at the conference, even as observers.[22] France denied a visa to Kurdish spokesman Hoshyar Zebari to come to Paris during the conference, and Zebari was reduced to issuing a statement in London on the eve of the conference, calling for international action against Iraq.[23] The United States failed, during and after the conference, even to take up the issue of amending the 1925 Protocol to bar states explicitly from using chemical weapons against their own citizens. A letter that Human Rights Watch sent Secretary of State Shultz on December 29, 1988, urging that the U.S. delegation raise this matter at the Paris conference went unanswered.

The 1989 Session of the U.N. Human Rights Commission

Despite Iraq's record of arbitrary detention, murder, and torture, the Reagan administration did not press for action against Iraq at the session of the United Nations Human Rights Commission in 1988. Even more surprising, at the commission's session in 1989 the Bush administration stood back and let others take the initiative in trying to call Iraq to account for its use of chemical weapons against its Kurdish population and for its other serious abuses. The United States did not join in sponsoring the strongly worded resolution put forward by twelve other Western states, which called for the appointment of a special rapporteur to "make a thorough study of the human rights situation in Iraq."[24]

This resolution was prompted not only by Iraq's use of chemical weapons against the Kurds but also by Western governments' concern over the commission's dismissal of a series of human rights complaints made against Iraq under the confidential procedure of Resolution 1503.[25] Most Western Euro-

pean delegates felt it important, in light of these developments, that some-
thing be done to call attention to the situation in Iraq. The United States,
however, evidently did not share this view.

A U.S. official told Middle East Watch that the State Department's instruc-
tions gave the U.S. delegation discretionary authority to sponsor the resolution but did not require it to do so. In a conversation with Middle East Watch,
a State Department official sought to justify the U.S. delegation's failure to
sponsor the resolution by claiming that doing so would have made the resolution an East-West issue and would have thereby diminished its chances of
success. Behind this unpersuasive rationale evidently lay at least two considerations. One was the fear that too heavy identification with the resolution
would detract from U.S. efforts, considered politically more important, to
obtain a resolution condemning Cuban human rights abuses. The other had to
do with U.S. bilateral relations with Iraq. There was, one official candidly
acknowledged to Middle East Watch, concern that U.S. sponsorship of the
resolution would be "too confrontational" toward Iraq.

On March 8, the Iraqi delegation moved under the rules of procedure to
block the Western resolution from coming to a vote. In the ensuing ballot, the
resolution was defeated 13 to 17. The United States joined its Western partners in opposing the Iraqi procedural motion but did not make the serious
lobbying effort that might have saved the resolution.

8

COVERING UP
HUMAN RIGHTS VIOLATIONS

The belief that the Iraqi government is "uniquely impervious to criticism on human rights issues"—a statement heard repeatedly from U.S. officials—is at best questionable. Our investigation has shown that the Iraqi government is sensitive to criticism on the grounds of human rights. It is prepared to go to extraordinary lengths to obscure its violations and to fend off censure. And while flouting its international human rights commitments, it aspires to establish for itself the reputation of a respectable and law-abiding member of the community of nations. Iraq has pursued these objectives quite relentlessly, with breathtaking disregard for its credibility. Its tools have been secrecy, intimidation, false and misleading claims, lobbying in international fora, and a public relations effort in the United States tutored by hired advocates and abetted by a growing business lobby.

DENIAL

The Iraqi government regularly and categorically denies that it commits any abuse—from torture, disappearance, and extrajudicial killing to the use of chemical weapons. It maintains that torture is not an officially sanctioned practice in Iraq and that when it occurs it is punished, although until 1989 a specific instance in which a torturer was brought to justice had never been cited.[1] Iraq has rejected the testimony of torture victims, even when it has been corroborated by independent medical examination or, as in the case of U.S. citizen Robert Spurling cited above, by diplomatic officials.[2] Iraq has repeatedly sought to dismiss the protests of human rights organizations over

115

disappearances and extrajudicial killings by denying knowledge of the abuses—as in the case of the disappearance of the 8,000 Barzani tribesmen[3]—or by advancing unsubstantiated claims that executions were carried out in full compliance with established judicial procedures. For years, the Iraqi government categorically and vehemently denied using poison gas against Iran, despite unimpeachable evidence documented by the United Nations. When Iraq finally acknowledged that it had used chemical weapons, in July 1988,[4] it defended its action by claiming the right to use any means to assure its survival. It denied and continues to deny having used chemical weapons against its Kurdish citizens, despite strong evidence that it did.

SECRECY AND INTIMIDATION

A heavy cloak of secrecy is employed to back Baghdad's denials. The Iraqi government has, so far, never allowed independent verification of charges of human rights violations.[5] In September 1988 it brusquely refused a request by U.N. Secretary General Perez de Cuellar, backed by the United States, the Soviet Union, and eleven other states, to investigate charges made by the United States and others that Iraq had used chemical weapons against the Kurds. Year after year, Iraq has ignored requests by the U.N. Human Rights Commission's Working Group on Disappearances for permission to visit Iraq. In 1988, evidently in exasperation, the Working Group pointedly drew the Iraqi government's attention to the fact that Human Rights Commission resolution 1988/34 and U.N. General Assembly resolution 42/142 encourage governments concerned with disappearances to give serious consideration to inviting the Working Group to visit their countries, and it added insistently that "a visit to Iraq would make an important contribution to its [the Working Group's] understanding of outstanding matters . . . within its mandate."[6] The Iraqi government ignored this request, as it had the earlier ones. In September 1988, Iraq turned down a request from the ICRC that might have permitted Iraqi Kurdish refugees in Turkey to come home. The Turkish government had asked the ICRC to undertake a large-scale program of repatriation for Iraqi Kurds who had fled poison-gas attacks in August and early September. The ICRC agreed to do so on condition that the Iraqi government guarantee the safety of those returning and allow the ICRC to oversee their resettlement. Although Iraq had announced an amnesty for the Kurdish refugees in Turkey and was urging them to return, it refused to give the guarantee requested or to allow the ICRC access to Iraqi territory, according to an ICRC official interviewed by Middle East Watch.

Human rights groups have fared little better than international organizations in gaining access to Iraq. Amnesty International was permitted to visit Baghdad in 1983 to confer with government officials but was not allowed to visit prisons or to travel outside the Iraqi capital. While on a visit to Baghdad in 1985 at the invitation of the Iraqi Women's Federation, Laurie Wiseberg, director of Human Rights Internet, was refused permission to visit prisons and other places of detention. As mentioned, Middle East Watch's own request to visit Iraq, received politely and even with expressions of sympathy by the Iraqi ambassador in Washington, met first with excuses and then with silence.

Western journalists who apply for visas to Iraq have had some better luck. In recent years they have been allowed to visit Iraq in increasing numbers, but in almost all cases strict limits have been placed on where they could go and whom they could see.

Inside Iraq the regime has imposed silence on its citizens. Iraqi émigrés often refuse to speak even anonymously of their government's human rights abuses for fear of retaliation, either against themselves in their place of asylum or against their relatives in Iraq. In two separate instances, Iraqis recently arrived in the United States first agreed to speak to Middle East Watch about conditions in Iraq but then changed their minds; one gave no reason while the other explained that he feared for the safety of his relatives at home. "If they ever found out," he said, "they would kill everyone." In another instance, an Iraqi student who first volunteered to give testimony failed to show up for the interview and did not answer later telephone calls. One prominent Iraqi dissident in exile who agreed to speak lives under death threat even in the West; he carries with him at all times a handwritten card identifying himself as a target for assassination by the Iraqi government.

Although as noted earlier the Iraqi government appears recently to have put a halt to assassinations in Britain, Iraqi refugees continue to live in fear of harassment by their government's agents and of the broad network of informers which, they say, is run by intelligence operatives attached to the London embassy. In May 1989, the *Guardian* reported that an exiled Iraqi Kurd, Hussein Haider, a British citizen for some years, had written to Prime Minister Thatcher appealing for her intervention to stop what he described as "a ruthless campaign of harassment and intimidation against him and his family by the Iraqi Government, both in Baghdad and London." Haidar complained that Iraqi agents in Britain had systematically tried to recruit him as an informer and that when he refused, family members in Iraq were first arrested and tortured and then, in April 1989, summarily deported to a refugee camp in Iran.[7] In an interview with Middle East Watch, an Iraqi opposition figure in Britain described the large Iraqi refugee population there—estimated at between 150,000 and 200,000—as frightened and cowed: "When they buy our paper off the newsstand they first look around to see if anybody is watching, then they snatch it and shove it deep inside their briefcase or coat so no one will know that they have it."

In the United States as well, Iraqi dissidents live in fear of surveillance by their government. Several sources interviewed by Middle East Watch said they believed that the Iraqi government maintains throughout the United States a network of informants—many of them disguised as students—to check and report on the loyalty of Iraqi students at U.S. institutions and on attitudes of Iraqi resident in the United States. One Iraqi student who defected while in the United States dropped out of an east coast university and enrolled in a school in the midwest, explaining to Middle East Watch that "there I can be safe, there are no other Iraqis out there." On arriving at his new school, he was surprised not only to find that there were other Iraqi students but to meet an Iraqi "graduate student," a man in his forties, who he believed was in charge of his government's surveillance program at that particular institution.

THE EFFORT TO MISLEAD

Iraq also misrepresents the human rights situation inside its borders in an effort to mislead world opinion. In 1986, a year in which the torture and murder of political prisoners reportedly continued unabated and Kurdish villages were being razed and their inhabitants sent off to detention camps, the Iraqi government reported to the Human Rights Committee established under the International Covenant on Civil and Political Rights that it was "making every effort to promote human rights."[8] In support of this statement, the Iraqi government advanced a number of claims that are either spurious or, because of their vagueness and Iraqi secrecy, impossible to verify. It claimed that "trade unions and other people's organizations contribute to the protection of human rights." The Bar Association, the Iraqi government report said, plays "a particularly important role in the protection of human rights" by assigning attorneys to defend persons who cannot afford to hire counsel and by "drafting and enforcing of legislation concerning human rights."

This same Iraqi government report stated that human rights "are taught as a higher educational subject in the Faculty of Law and Politics at the University of Baghdad," and that "students are encouraged to engage in research and to prepare university theses on human rights." It claimed that "a significant role is also played by the Human Rights Association in Iraq which makes representations to the authorities concerned with a view to dealing with complaints received from individuals or organizations."

Denied access to Iraq, Middle East Watch was unable to check on the role of the trade unions and the Bar Association or to determine whether, and if so how, human rights are actually taught at the Baghdad University Law Faculty. But the Human Rights Association seemed another matter. From the description given in the Iraqi government's report, it seemed legitimate to suppose that the association should be a well-known and well-regarded organization. Middle East Watch was for some time unable to find any trace of an organization called The Human Rights Association in Iraq. When asked, State Department officials who had served in Iraq or worked in Washington on Iraqi affairs said they had never heard of a group by this name. Human Rights Internet, an organization whose specific purpose is to catalog and correspond with human rights organizations throughout the world, had no record of it; neither did the United Nations Human Rights Center Information Office in New York. A letter sent to the Iraqi ambassador in Washington asking for the address of the Human Rights Association in Iraq and the name of its director went unanswered. Later inquiries finally confirmed that there was in fact such an organization. From all that could be learned, it exists only in name, and although it claims to be a private organization, it reportedly is headed by a government official.

Many other examples can be cited of the Iraqi government's practice of deliberate misrepresentation. A few have already been mentioned: the incomplete and misleading information on Iraq's death penalty laws provided to the Human Rights Committee in the Iraqi government's report submitted in April 1986;[9] Ambassador Nizar Hamdoon's letter of July 11, 1985, assuring that Drs. Hussain Shahristani and Jaafar Dhia Jaafar had been pardoned and released a "long time ago," when in fact nothing had been heard from either in many years and Dr. Shahristani was still in prison;[10] and the statement issued by Iraqi ambassadors on June 26, 1989, alleging that depopulation and resettlement measures were being applied only to a corridor along Iraq's borders with Turkey and Iran.[11]

Another tactic employed by Iraqi envoys from time to time is the issuance of spurious invitations to visit Iraq and investigate human rights conditions there. In September 1988 the Iraqi ambassador in London, Mohammed Sadiq al-Mashat, invited three British Members of Parliament to visit Iraq. After they asked to go to Kurdish areas and to visit prisons, and to question Iraqi officials on human rights, their visit was "postponed," prompting one of the MPs to comment that "if the regime has nothing to hide, if it is really a 'stable country,' . . . why were we not allowed to visit Iraq?"[12] In the spring of 1989, Lord Avebury, chairman of the Parliamentary Human Rights Group (PHRG), wrote three times to Ambassador al-Mashat asking for the Iraqi government's agreement to a visit by a PHRG delegation. The ambassador never replied in writing but did agree to meet with PHRG members. In the course of the meeting on July 20, 1989, according to the PHRG minutes, the Iraqi envoy asserted that "we are undergoing a process of democratization, yes we are, slowly but surely"; claimed that "there is now a liberalization of travel" abroad for Iraqis; and announced that "the media will no longer be controlled under the new press law." On the matter of a visit to Iraq, Ambassador al-Mashat stated that if a parliamentary delegation wished to visit Iraq, "they could go anywhere they liked. . . . They could have their own interpreter for the trip." Immediately following the meeting, Lord Avebury wrote to the ambassador to take up the offer to visit Iraq. Ambassador al-Mashat departed Britain in August 1989 without having answered Lord Avebury's letter.[13] The Parliamentary Human Rights Group is still awaiting a reply.

Although Iraq is a party to the International Covenant on Civil and Political Rights, it occasionally has fallen back on the argument that its treatment of its citizens is an internal matter and that concern with human rights in Iraq is interference in Iraq's internal affairs. When Amnesty International inquired, during its mission to Baghdad in January 1983, about laws that levy the death penalty for political acts related to membership in the Baath party, it was told that the question concerned the party's internal affairs and was none of Amnesty's business. When asked by Western journalists in September 1988 about the U.N. secretary general's proposal to send a team to investigate charges that chemical weapons had been used against the Kurds, Iraq's defense minister dismissed the idea as an infringement of Iraq's sovereignty and added ominously, "I want to deal with a certain segment of my population in the way I want." [14] When midlevel state department officials received Kurdish rebel leader Jalal Talabani during his visit to Washington in June 1988, the Iraqi government accused the United States of interference in its internal affairs. In response, the State Department lent legitimacy to the Iraqi claim by declaring defensively: "The United States does not interfere in the internal affairs of those countries." [15]

FIGHTING OFF CENSURE IN INTERNATIONAL FORA

Deflecting censure of their government's policies is one of the main objectives of Iraqi representatives at international organizations, one to which an extraordinary amount of time and energy is devoted. The Iraqi delegation at the United Nations in New York made frantic, albeit unsuccessful, efforts to fend off U.N. resolutions condemning the use of poison gas in the Iran-Iraq War. In one instance, in July 1988, Iraqi diplomats reportedly even attempted to interfere in the work of the U.N.'s Arabic translation service in an effort to delay publication of a U.N. report of an investigation into Iraq's use of chemical weapons. [16]

The Iraqi mission in Geneva, venue of the United Nations Human Rights Commission, is in the front line of efforts to prevent Baghdad from being called to account for its human rights abuses. Over the years Iraq has sought and repeatedly won election to the commission, and it has participated aggressively in the commission's debates even when it has not held membership. Western officials who are familiar with the commission's work say that Iraqi representatives never allow any criticism of their government's human rights policies to go unanswered, and that Iraq's delegation is always among the largest and most active of those in attendance at the commission's annual sessions. As mentioned in chapter 6, during the commission's session in 1989 the Iraqi delegation succeeded in defeating, on a procedural motion, a Western resolution that expressed concern over reports of chemical-weapons use against the Kurds and called for the appointment of a special rapporteur to study the human rights situation in Iraq. The Iraqi delegation also succeeded in quashing commission action on Iraq under the confidential procedure of resolution 1503. Iraq was one of eight countries recommended by the Subcommission on Prevention of Discrimination and Protection of Minorities for consideration by the Human Rights Commission. The Iraqi delegation, however, mustered the votes needed to get the commission to reject the subcommission's recommendation.[17] In August 1989, Iraq's observer delegation to the annual meeting of the subcommission succeeded, through intensive lobbying, in killing a resolution sponsored by eight of the subcommission's independent experts recommending that the Human Rights Commission, in its session of February–March 1990, "study carefully . . . the evolution of the situation of human rights and fundamental freedoms in Iraq."[18]

In these and other instances, Western officials say, Iraqi diplomats have aggressively and skillfully lobbied Third World and Soviet bloc delegations, invoking Arab, Islamic, and nonaligned solidarity, trading votes, and playing heavily on the reluctance of certain Latin American governments to support censure of other states on human rights grounds.

Since 1988, the Iraqi mission in Geneva has been headed by Barzan al-Takriti, half-brother of President Saddam Hussein and former head of the Baath Party General Intelligence Directorate, a vicious secret police. His appointment to head the Iraqi delegation to the Human Rights Commission is seen by members of many other delegations as a mark of Iraq's scorn for the commission and for human rights generally.

SELLING THE NEW IRAQ

Parallel to its efforts to stifle criticism, the Iraqi government in recent years has sought to remake its public image abroad by promoting the idea of "a new Iraq"—not one of torture, summary execution, poison gas, and forced resettlement but one where concern for human rights and democracy are beginning to take root.

The United States has been the focus of the Iraqi government's effort to etch itself a more alluring profile. Iraq's enormous oil wealth, its ambitious postwar redevelopment program and the prospect of lucrative trade predispose an important segment of American opinion in its favor.[19] The Iraqi government has been helped in reinforcing that predisposition by American business consultants who specialize in the promotion of trade with Arab countries. The United States–Iraq Business Forum, established in 1985 in Washington, serves as a kind of chamber of commerce for U.S. firms that want to do business with Iraq. It has sought to generate favorable publicity for Iraq, to make that country's economic potential known to American firms and to help them obtain contracts and establish joint ventures. It has also worked to mobilize U.S. firms to oppose congressionally mandated sanctions against Iraq for human rights violations. When in October 1989 the Senate put a rider on the Foreign Assistance Act barring the Export-Import Bank from doing business with Iraq, the United States–Iraq Business Forum reportedly sent messages to its member firms—some of them among the largest U.S. corporations—urging them to lobby against the measure. Congressional committees were deluged by calls and cables of protest.[20]

In June 1989, the United States–Iraq Business Forum organized a visit to Baghdad for executives of thirteen major U.S. banks and corporations. The highlight of the visit was a cordial two-hour meeting with President Saddam Hussein in which he described Iraq as "undergoing a process of economic privatization and political reform" and emphasized his desire to strengthen commercial links with the United States.[21] The red carpet was rolled out for the group during its three-day stay in Baghdad. Meetings with President Hussein and other senior officials were accorded top play in the Iraqi media, in an apparent effort to send the message to more junior Iraqi officials and businessmen that they could now meet with U.S. businessmen without fear of being hauled in by the police for questioning.

In 1985 the Iraqi embassy in Washington hired a U.S. public relations firm, Edward J. Van Kloberg and Associates, to help revamp its public image. Ambassador Nizar Hamdoon agreed to pay the firm $1,000 for "every interview with [a] distinguished American newspaper" that could be arranged.[22] Van Kloberg and Associates have, by their own report, arranged television interviews and placed articles favorable to Iraq in major U.S. newspapers, including *The Washington Post, The Washington Times, The Wall Street Journal*, and *The New York Times*. Among its list of activities on behalf of the Iraqi government during 1987, Van Kloberg claimed credit for an op-ed piece in *The New York Times* of August 27 signed by Congressman Les Aspin, chairman of the House Armed Services Committee, advocating that the United States retaliate against Iran's mining of international waters in the Persian Gulf by mining Iranian waters, a clear act of war.[23] In May 1986 the Iraqi embassy hired a Washington law firm, Paul, Hastings, Janofsky and Walker, "to provide counseling and analysis relevant to United States policies of interest to the Government of the Republic of Iraq, and . . . to assist in arrang-

ing and preparing for meetings with United States elected and appointed officials."[24] Paul, Hastings, Janofsky and Walker has reported to the U.S. Justice
Department that between May 1986 and December 1988 it received a total of
$131,847 from the Iraqi government for these services.[25]

Iraq's effort to remake its public image has faced considerably greater ob-
stacles in the United Kingdom. Because Britain was the colonial power, and
perhaps because of the substantial number of Iraqis who have sought asylum
in the U.K., the British public is well informed about Iraq and concerned
about human rights violations there. British press coverage of Iraq is relatively comprehensive and has been almost uniformly critical.[26] There appears
to be no identifiable Iraqi lobby, friendship society, or chamber of commerce
in the U.K.; whether the Iraqi government has engaged a public-relations or
lobbying firm to advance its interests in the U.K. cannot be known since
British law does not require disclosure of such activities. The British government has denounced Iraq's use of chemical weapons and pressed resolutions
critical of Iraq in both the U.N. Human Rights Commission and the European
Community. It takes credit for having inspired the writing of a report on
human rights in Iraq by European Community ambassadors in Baghdad in
June 1989. And it prides itself, in its own words, on seizing "every opportunity to put pressure on the Iraqis bilaterally" concerning their human rights
abuses.[27]

Not, however, where trade is at issue. British export credits to Iraq for
manufactured goods currently surpass those of any other Western country.
Although overall figures for British credits to Iraq have not been made public,
one expert interviewed by Middle East Watch who requested anonymity estimated that they totalled 2.5 billion pounds—or over 4 billion dollars—from
1984 to 1988. In 1989, the year following its public rebuke of Iraq for using
chemical weapons against the Kurds, the British government reportedly doubled its export credit line to Baghdad.[28] Unlike the United States, which has
placed an embargo on the sale of all military supplies to Iraq, Britain sells
"nonlethal" equipment to Baghdad. The Thatcher government allowed British arms makers to display their wares at a Baghdad arms exposition in the
summer of 1989. In August 1989, however, the British government turned
down a request from Iraq for the purchase of some sixty Hawk trainer aircraft,
and it cited concern over human rights as one of the main reasons.

The Baath regime's efforts to woo the Western media date from the beginning of the 1980s. Within days after it launched its war against Iran, in Sep-

tember 1980, the Iraqi government invited hundreds of foreign journalists to witness the anticipated victory. The victory failed to arrive on schedule and the experience of dealing with the unruly and irreverent representatives of a free press left a bitter aftertaste. Rules for entry were tightened, and some years passed before the Iraqi government began again to experiment with opening its doors to the Western press.

Over the past two years or so, foreign journalists have once again been allowed into Iraq with greater frequency, albeit still under strict governmental control. In a few cases this access has produced stories favorable to the regime—notably articles in the *New Yorker* by journalist Milton Viorst[29]—but overall the results must have been disappointing. Most of the reports filed by Western journalists following visits to Iraq have been critical, some scathingly and even satirically so, as in the case of a story carried by the Madrid newspaper *El Pais* on the cult of the personality of the Iraqi president headlined "Saddam the Ubiquitous."[30] The Iraqi government's attempts to control Western reporters' activities could hardly be expected to predispose them in its favor. As noted, one American journalist who visited Iraq in the summer of 1989 related that she was lodged in a room in the luxury Al-Rashid hotel in which there were videocameras both in the room and in the bathroom. When she filed a story to an editor in the United States she found that it had been entirely rewritten by the Iraqi censor.[31]

The success rate with U.S. foreign policy intellectuals has been much higher. Two books favorable to Iraq's government have been published in the 1980s by U.S. writers associated with Washington think tanks, Christine Moss Helms's *Iraq: Eastern Flank of the Arab World*[32] and Fredrick W. Axelgard's *A New Iraq?*[33] Under the impetus of its director of Middle East studies, former U.S. Ambassador Robert G. Neumann, the Center for International and Strategic Studies in Washington has organized activities—with the "generous and consistent financial support" of a number of corporations and foundations—with the purpose of underscoring "the significance of the many opportunities that the future holds should U.S.–Iraqi relations stabilize on their present upward course."[34]

The Iraqi government has also acquired greater sophistication in matters of public relations. It has continued to bar access to its territory to human rights organizations but has thrown the door open to groups known to be sympathetic. For example, in September 1989, while Middle East Watch waited for a reply to its request—made three months earlier—to visit Iraq, the Iraqi embassy in Washington invited a delegation of American academics and businesspeople to attend ceremonies at the restored site of Babylon and to tour the country. A group of British parliamentarians and British and French journalists were also invited to witness elections in the Kurdish Autonomous Region in September 1989, an event hailed by the Iraqi government as a major exercise in democracy.

To favored writers and to visiting Western business executives and political figures, Iraqi officials have dropped tantalizing hints of coming liberalization in their country's political system—of the prospect of a new constitution, of freely functioning opposition newspapers and political parties, of measures to provide further public freedoms, of the strengthening of the authority of the National Assembly, and even of the possible abolition of the Revolutionary Command Council. One U.S. foreign policy intellectual, a frequent visitor to Baghdad, hailed these reforms as possibly being "a significant watershed in the history of Iraq's politics," if put into effect.[35]

The enthusiasm seems premature. Iraqi officials have told recent visitors and foreign officials they meet on their trips abroad that the new constitution, which they say is nearing approval, will guarantee freedom of expression and a multiparty system.[36] But so far, despite this and other talk of liberalization, no step of any significance has been taken. In fact, as the writer quoted above has acknowledged, a change made in February 1989 in the law governing membership in the National Assembly was clearly retrogressive; to an earlier requirement that candidates for the assembly need not be members of the Baath party but must support the principles of the July 17–30 "revolution" was added the further stipulation that candidates must have made "effective, original contributions toward the sacred battle against the Iranian aggression."[37]

Despite this tightening of the rules, the National Assembly elections held in April 1989 were put on international display in an effort to show that democracy had arrived, or was arriving, in Iraq. A delegation of British Members of Parliament was invited to witness the elections and British journalists were given free run of the polling places. Correspondents reported no evidence of poll rigging, but neither did they see signs of genuine change in the air—undoubtedly a reflection of the lack of freedom of expression and association needed to make elections meaningful. "Ordinary Iraqis," one journalist reported, "have no expectations that things are about to change radically after 20 years of despotic rule. . . . 'This election is designed simply to bolster the regime, not to change it.' "[38]

The elections to the Kurdish assembly of September 1989 got an even more caustic review from a French journalist invited to witness them. Le Monde's correspondent wrote:

> If one didn't find any polling booths in Iraqi Kurdistan during the elections held there on September 9, if numerous ballots of Kurds presented as illiterate were filled out directly by the scrutineers or if the latter kept a watchful eye on the ballots filled out—in public—by more educated electors, it was for no other reason than to facilitate the citizen's task. To see in this some distortion of the democratic practices in effect under other latitudes would be only pure malice.[39]

What all this adds up to is that the Iraqi government does indeed care what the world thinks of it. President Saddam Hussein appeared to acknowledge this when, in a speech on November 28, 1988, he announced an amnesty for political offenders and declared: "I do not say that we respect and care for human rights as we really wish in Iraq. I cannot claim that human rights are respected the way I wish and want. However, with God's help we will reach the stage that will satisfy us and you."[40] The Iraqi government's sensitivity to world opinion may offer the best hope for bringing about genuine change in its human rights policies. Governments and human rights organizations will have to continue to call Iraq to account for its abuses, to expose its denials and its false and misleading statements, and to beware of its attempts to seduce international opinion through public relations and influence peddling. Persistence will be required to press the Iraqi government to respect the commitments it has freely taken upon itself in its own laws and through its ratification of international human rights covenants. Silence, in the mistaken belief that the Iraqi government is impervious to criticism, will not suffice.

9

CONCLUSIONS AND
RECOMMENDATIONS

Iraq is a well-organized police state and its government is one of the most brutal and repressive regimes in power today. With the exception of freedom of worship, the Iraqi government denies its citizens all fundamental rights and freedoms, and ruthlessly suppresses even the smallest gestures of dissent. Iraqi citizens enjoy neither freedom of expression nor freedom to form or join political parties or trade unions of their choice. Their government subjects them to forced relocation and deportation, arbitrary arrest and detention, torture, disappearance, and summary and political execution. There is no meaningful legal recourse in Iraq against these abuses.

The Iraqi government imposes its rule through:

the Baath party's monolithic organization, which penetrates all elements of society and is responsible for enforcing political and social conformity;

a pervasive system of informing—such that Iraq has become a nation of informers—which denies Iraqis the right to express their views candidly, even in private, and encourages friends and family members to report on one another;

a highly developed cult of personality for President Saddam Hussein, active participation in which has become a test of loyalty and a prerequisite for advancement;

secret-police agencies that are empowered to arrest, detain without trial, torture, and kill.

The Iraqi government has perpetrated these abuses in flagrant violation of its own constitution and law; the International Covenant on Civil and Political

Rights, to which it is a party; and the Declaration on the Protection of All Persons from Being Subjected to Torture or other Cruel, Inhuman or Degrading Treatment or Punishment, with which it has declared itself in voluntary compliance.

Before and during the war with Iran, the Iraqi government arbitrarily and forcibly deported to Iran many tens of thousands—as many as two or three hundred thousand by some accounts—after stripping them of all property. Many of those deported were Iraqi citizens. The Iraqi government has refused to take responsibility for these deportees or to allow their repatriation since the end of the war.

The Iraqi government regularly employed chemical weapons in its war against Iran, and in the last year and a half of that war, turned these outlawed weapons against its own Kurdish population—insurgent guerrilla fighters and civilians alike. During the war, the Iraqi government summarily executed Kurdish civilians in reprisal for attacks perpetrated by Kurdish guerrillas. Since 1987, on the pretext of protecting the Kurdish population and providing them modern amenities, the Iraqi government has expelled several hundred thousand Kurds from their mountain villages and towns, razed their dwellings and obliged them to resettle in "new towns" in hot dry lowlands where they find little if any way to provide for themselves. The Iraqi government has destroyed, according to one conservative estimate, some 1,200 Kurdish villages and towns—places where Kurds have lived for centuries or millennia—and large segments of traditionally Kurdish areas of Iraq have been emptied of population.

For some time the Iraqi government has been conducting a public-relations campaign in the United States, advised and assisted by public-relations firms and legal counsel. The campaign is designed to try to cover up abuses and to give the Iraqi government an appearance of respectability, but at the same time the government has continued the brutal repression of its citizens. This campaign has been abetted by U.S. organizations interested in promoting trade and better political relations between the United States and Iraq.

The Reagan and Bush administrations professed concern over the human rights situation in Iraq, but except in the matter of chemical weapons (and even there with no consistency), gave Iraqi abuses no more than scant attention. Both administrations put the nurturing of new friendly relations with the Iraqi government well ahead of human rights considerations. In recent years, despite Iraq's use of chemical weapons against its Kurdish population and other extensive violent abuses, the United States has resumed its Export-Import Bank credit guarantees to Iraq and extended billions of dollars to the Iraqi government in credit guarantees for the purchase of U.S. agricultural products. Although the United States denounced the poison-gas attacks, it has never spoken out against Iraq's policy of forced relocation of its Kurdish population, even though other Western governments have issued public protests, and it has given only lukewarm support to Western government efforts to call Iraq to account before the United Nations Human Rights Commission.

The recommendations of Middle East Watch fall into three categories.

THE IRAQI GOVERNMENT

The Iraqi government should respect the human rights guarantees contained in its own constitution and laws and should honor the commitments it has taken upon itself in ratifying the International Covenant on Civil and Political Rights. It should cease all practices—arbitrary arrest and detention, torture, extralegal killing, disappearance, deportation, and forced relocation—that violate the Covenant and other commonly recognized human rights standards.

The following are specific steps the Iraqi government could take immediately to show a good-faith effort to improve its human rights record:

Repeal all laws that stipulate the death penalty or prison sentences for acts that are purely political in nature, in particular the 1986 law that stipulates life imprisonment or the death penalty for "insult" to the president of the Republic or the senior institutions of state. Death-penalty laws pertaining to Baath party members and current or former members of the military and security forces who join other parties should also be repealed. Review all death-penalty laws with a view to reducing their number and repealing those that do not accord with the provision of Article 6 of the Covenant which stipulates that "sentence of death may be imposed only for the most serious crimes."

Allow international organizations and private human rights groups access to its territory to investigate charges of human rights violations and to verify human rights conditions.

Release all prisoners held for their peaceful expression or association, as well as family members detained in lieu of persons sought by the authorities, or detained in retaliation for their flight.

Enter into talks with authentic spokesmen for the Kurdish minority, with a view to agreeing on arrangements that would permit Kurdish citizens who have been forcibly relocated or interned to return to their homes and resume a normal life.

Make arrangements to allow Iraqi citizens who were deported before and during the war with Iran to begin to return to their homes.

Set up a commission to examine complaints of persons tortured and illegally detained, and pay compensation to them and to families of persons murdered by the security forces.

Prosecute and punish those responsible for such gross violations as execution, disappearance, and torture.

THE UNITED STATES GOVERNMENT

Until such time as the Iraqi government takes steps to show sincere and meaningful progress toward respect of the fundamental rights of its citizens:

All Commodity Credit Corporation and Export-Import Bank credits should be terminated.

Export from the United States to Iraq of any product or technology that could contribute to Iraq's military capabilities or arms development and production effort, or to the maintenance or strengthening of Iraq's internal security forces, should be banned.

In addition:

The Bush administration should publicly and repeatedly condemn the Iraqi government for the sorts of gross abuses described in the annual report on human rights in Iraq, including summary and political execution, disappearance, torture, prolonged political imprisonment, and the forced relocation of the Kurds.

Congress should conduct public hearings on human rights violations in Iraq, calling as witnesses, among others, persons who have suffered torture, chemical-weapons poisoning, and other grave abuses at the hands of the Iraqi government.

The State Department, should sponsor, speak out for, actively support, and lobby for resolutions in the United Nations, in particular in the Commission on Human Rights and, to the extent appropriate, in the General Assembly, of resolutions censuring Iraq for its consistent gross violations of human rights.

The State Department, through the U.S. ambassador in Baghdad and senior U.S. officials in Washington, should also seek to engage the Iraqi government in a dialogue on these human rights concerns.

The United States should eschew any measure or action that would, directly or indirectly, give political, economic, scientific, technological, military, or strategic support to Iraq, until such time as the Iraqi government dramatically curbs abuses.

THE INTERNATIONAL COMMUNITY

The international community should bring pressure to bear on the Iraqi government, through economic and political means, to persuade it to cease its violations of fundamental human rights and to accept international verification of its human rights practices.

All governments should support resolutions in the United Nations, in the Commission on Human Rights and elsewhere, condemning Iraq's human rights violations. Iraq should be pressed to observe the Universal Declaration of Human Rights and to honor its commitments under the International Covenant on Civil and Political Rights.

The United Nations and its various agencies, commissions and committees should initiate studies of human rights in Iraq and pursue efforts to gain access to Iraq for on-the-spot verification of human rights conditions.

The United Nations High Commissioner for Refugees (UNHCR) should take immediate steps, in coordination with the International Committee of the Red Cross (ICRC) to the extent appropriate, to offer assistance to the up to 200,000 Iraqi citizens deported to Iran before and during the Iran-Iraq War. UNHCR and ICRC should press the Iraqi government to allow repatriation of these persons and oversee such repatriation to assure that the rights of all those who return are fully respected.

NOTES

INTRODUCTION

1. Hanna Batatu, "Iraq's Underground Shi'i Movements," *Middle East Reports* (January 1982), p. 7. In Arabic the two words are alliterative, *tarhib* (terror) and *targhib* (reward).

2. In a speech delivered on November 28, 1988, before the Arab Lawyers Union, for example, President Saddam Hussein declared: "I cannot claim that human rights are respected [in Iraq] the way I wish and want. . . . However, with God's help we will reach the stage that will satisfy us and you."

3. In August 1989, at the end of the session of the U.N. Human Rights Commission's Subcommission on Prevention of Discrimination and Protection of Minorities, the Iraqi delegate invited members of the subcommission to visit his country to look into charges of chemical-weapons use against the Kurdish population and forced resettlement of the Kurds. Because this invitation was issued orally and in the course of debate over a resolution censuring Iraq for these abuses, the offer was viewed by many as a tactical move designed to forestall passage of the resolution. No written invitation is known ever to have been issued, and the terms under which the visit would occur were never specified. A visit to Iraq by the members of the subcommission would be welcome, but as this report went to press there was no indication that one would take place.

4. An amendment to the Iraqi Penal Code introduced in 1984 prescribes the death penalty for "[w]hoever works with a foreign state or with anyone working in its interest or communicates with either of them, resulting in damage to the military, political or economic position of Iraq." Article 164(1).

5. Western diplomatic personnel in Baghdad find that, as in most police states, there is a small number of Iraqis who seem both ready and eager to mix socially with them. These people are usually easily recognized as informers whose fraternization is officially authorized and who report directly to one or more of the security services.

CHAPTER I: BACKGROUND

1. Ismet Sheriff Vanly, writing in Gerard Chaliand, ed., *People Without a Country* (London: Zed Press, 1982), p. 157, calculates that in 1975 the Kurds numbered 3.0 million, or some 28 percent of Iraq's population. The Minority Rights Group, in a

report entitled "The Kurds," published in March 1989, estimates that Iraq's Kurds numbered 3,105,000 in 1980, or 23 percent of the Iraqi population in that year.

2. This is the estimate given by historian Phebe Marr in *The Modern History of Iraq* (Boulder, Colorado: Westview Press, 1985), p. 5.

3. For more on the history of the Kurds in Iraq, see chap. 5.

4. Marr, *The Modern History of Iraq*, p. 163.

5. Marion and Peter Sluglett, *Iraq Since 1958* (London: KPI, 1987), p. 86.

6. A U.N. mission on visit to prisoner-of-war camps in Iraq in August 1988 reported: "We also saw young POWs among them, starting at age 13, who had been part of the Iranian army." (Report of the Mission Dispatched by the Secretary General on the Situation of Prisoners of War in the Islamic Republic of Iran and Iraq, UNSC Document S/20174, August 24, 1988, pp. 24–25.)

7. *New York Times*, September 19, 1988.

8. *New York Times*, September 23, 1985.

9. *Boston Globe*, September 22, 1985.

10. Donald Kirk, *The New Republic*, February 22, 1988, p. 11.

11. See Milton Viorst, "The View from the Mustansiriyah," *The New Yorker*, October 12, 1987. Viorst remarked that the Iraqi capital "has made a calculated decision to let the war disturb its composure as little as possible." The calculated decision, of course, was made not by the citizens of Baghdad but by the Iraqi government.

12. Middle East Watch interview with Professor Amazia Baram, Woodrow Wilson Fellow, July 1989.

CHAPTER 2: THE INSTITUTIONS OF REPRESSION

1. Middle East Watch interviews with U.S. officials. See also Christine Moss Helms, *Iraq: Eastern Flank of the Arab World* (Washington, D.C.: The Brookings Institution, 1984), p. 131.

2. Adeed Dawisha, "The Politics of War," in Frederick W. Axelgard, ed., *Iraq in Transition* (Boulder, Colorado: Westview Press, 1986), p. 26.

3. Revolutionary Command Council resolution no. 1357 of November 10, 1971 prescribes the death penalty for "[a]ll military personnel participating in a prohibited political organization or carrying out prohibited political activity with the purpose of recruiting or spreading principles or trends detrimental to the [Baath party]." In 1976, this prohibition was amplified by an RCC resolution calling for the death penalty for "[a]ny activity or political organization within the ranks of the Iraqi armed forces which is detrimental to the Baath party." (Amnesty International, "The Death Penalty in Iraq," May 21, 1987.)

4. Over the years, there have been regular reports of Iraqi officers having been executed for allegedly plotting against the regime. Although it has been impossible to determine the validity of such charges, the Iraqi regime has commonly used accusations of coup plotting to purge opponents in the military and the party. See Frederick

W. Axelgard, "A New Iraq?" *The Washington Papers* (Washington, D.C.: Center for Strategic and International Studies, 1988), pp. 50–51.

5. Hanna Batatu, *The Old Social Classes and the Revolutionary Movements of Iraq* (Princeton, N.J.: Princeton Univ. Press, 1978), p. 1010.

6. This figure is cited by, among others, Marr, *The Modern History of Iraq*, p. 227.

7. *Le Monde*, January 7–8, 1979, cited in *Middle East Contemporary Survey 1978–79* (Boulder, Colorado: Westview Press), p. 566. Also see chap. 4.

8. The figure of 25,000 is cited by Marr, *The Modern History of Iraq*, p. 227; that of 50,000 is given in the U.S. State Department's *Country Reports on Human Rights Practices for 1988*, Iraq, p. 1362.

9. Helms, *Iraq*, pp. 83–86. In Baath party terminology, each individual Arab state is a "Region" within the "Arab Nation." Thus the Regional Command has jurisdiction over the "Iraqi Region." On the organizational charts the top body is the National Command, but its authority is only theoretical. In practice it handles relations with those Baath parties outside Iraq that maintain affiliation with the Iraqi Baath party. The National Command was headed by Michel Aflaq, one of the Baath's three founding fathers, until his death in June 1989. In deference to Aflaq, Saddam Hussein took a second seat in the National Command, with the title of Deputy Secretary General. Aflaq was an early supporter of Hussein and helped him win appointment to the Iraqi Regional Command in 1964. Hussein repaid the favor by giving Aflaq asylum, a job, and a title in Baghdad after he fled Syria in the 1960s.

10. Helms, *Iraq*, p. 91.

11. Samir Al-Khalil, *Republic of Fear* (Berkeley and Los Angeles: University of California Press, 1989), p. 33.

12. Middle East Watch interview with Professor Amazia Baram, July 1989.

13. Helms, *Iraq*, p. 83. This passage is given in quotation marks and is attributed by Helms to "a number of Ba'th and non-Ba'th Iraqis."

14. Al-Khalil, *Republic of Fear*, pp. 61–63, gives a vivid picture of the pervasiveness of informers in Baath Iraq and its corrosive effect on personal and social relationships.

15. *Index on Censorship*, October 1987.

16. *The New York Times*, April 3, 1984.

17. Revolutionary Command Council resolution 884, July 3, 1978, as cited in Amnesty International, "The Death Penalty in Iraq: Legal Aspects," May 21, 1987.

18. Para 1(a), Art. 200, Iraqi Penal Code. Amnesty International, "The Death Penalty in Iraq."

19. Law no. 107 of 1974. Amnesty International, "The Death Penalty in Iraq."

20. Law no. 145 of 1976. Amnesty International, "The Death Penalty in Iraq."

21. Law no. 111 of 1978. Amnesty International, "The Death Penalty in Iraq."

22. See, for example, Ronald Payne, "The Mad, Mad World of Saddam Hussein," *Telegraph Magazine* (London), November 18, 1989.

23. This is disputed by some sources who say that Saddam Hussein was in fact treated for his wound by Dr. Tahseen Muallah. Dr. Muallah fled Baath Iraq in 1977.

24. Fuad Mattar, *Saddam Hussein: The Man, the Cause and the Future*, (London: Third World Press, 1981), pp. 32–44. Amir Iskander, in *Saddam Hussein, the Fighter, the Thinker and the Man* (Paris: Hachette, 1980), pp. 60–73, tells an identical tale. Both books are officially sponsored biographies.

25. See Al-Khalil, *Republic of Fear*, p. 70. Most Iraqi exiles seem to share this suspicion. In their writings, however, Western authors generally credit the story that the transfer of power was amicable.

26. Marr, *The Modern History of Iraq*, p. 230.

27. Marion and Peter Sluglett, *Iraq Since 1958* (London: KPI, 1987), p. 209, citing *Die Zeit*, August 7, 1979.

28. Al-Khalil, *Republic of Fear*, p. 70.

29. Marr, *The Modern History of Iraq*, p. 231.

30. Quoted in *U.S. News and World Report*, September 25, 1989, p. 37.

31. Mattar, *Saddam Hussein*, and Iskander, *Saddam Hussein, the Fighter, the Thinker and the Man*.

32. *Middle East Contemporary Survey 1982–83* (Boulder, Colorado: Westview Press, for the Shiloah Institute, Tel Aviv University, 1982–83), pp. 565–66, from Baghdad daily *Al Thawra*, December 16, 1982.

33. Staff Report to the Committee on Foreign Relations, U.S. Senate, "War in the Persian Gulf: The US Takes Sides" (Washington, D.C.: U.S. Government Printing Office, 1987), p. 19.

34. Government officials, of course, must set an example of dedication. When Middle East Watch's representative visited the office of the Iraqi ambassador in Washington in June 1989, it was adorned by no less than three likenesses of President Saddam Hussein: two large portraits hung on the walls and a third framed and positioned on the ambassador's desk where ordinarily one might expect to see a family photograph.

35. Quoted in *Index on Censorship*, March 1988, p. 3, from Iraq's Official Gazette, no. 1324.

36. Reported in *Index on Censorship*, March 1988.

37. *The Sun* (London), September 8, 1981. For further details on Worth's case, see chap. 4.

38. For example, when members of a U.S. congressional delegation led by Representatives Mel Levine and Robert Torricelli, on a visit to Baghdad in January 1988, asked to visit the city's only synagogue, they were astounded to find themselves accompanied by a squad of fearsome looking, submachine-gun-toting agents whose purpose seemed less to protect the visitors than to intimidate anyone they might encounter.

39. Al-Khalil, *Republic of Fear*, chap. 1.

40. Al-Khalil, *Republic of Fear*, pp. 14–15.

41. All the above figures are from Al Khalil, *Republic of Fear*, p. 37, who cites as his source the 1976 and 1978 Annual Abstract of Statistics, Baghdad, Ministry of Planning.

42. Al-Khalil, *Republic of Fear*, pp. 37–38; and other experts consulted by Middle East Watch.

43. *The Times* (London), July 28, 1978.

44. *The Times* (London), February 9, 1978; *Surrey Comet*, February 11, 1978.

45. *Guardian* (London), March 9 and 13, 1979.

46. Helms, *Iraq*, p. 79, attributes these expulsions to the students having been caught distributing anti-Baathist literature.

47. Barry Rubin, ed., *The Politics of Terrorism* (Washington, D.C.: Foreign Policy Institute, School of Advanced International Studies, Johns Hopkins University, 1989), p. 58. According to this account, the attempt on Argov's life (he survived but was paralyzed) was carried out with the intent of creating tension between Israel and Syria. Three days later Israel invaded Lebanon and clashed with Syrian troops.

48. *The Times* (London), August 1, 1980.

49. All the foregoing, except the Berlin attempt, were cited by the Organization of Human Rights in Iraq, a London-based émigré organization, in a communication dated July 21, 1987. Kurdish sources interviewed by Middle East Watch provided information on the attempt to bomb their meeting place in Berlin in 1980.

50. Middle East Watch interview with Dr. Abdul Wahab al-Hakim, nephew of Sayyed Mahdi al-Hakim, who was with Sayyed Mahdi in Khartoum and was himself wounded in the attack; also unpublished letter from Lord Avebury, chairman, Parliamentary Human Rights Group, to Danilo Turk, U.N. Sub-Commission on Prevention of Discrimination and Protection of Minorities.

51. Gerard Chaliand, ed., *People without a Country* (London: Zed Press, 1980/82), p. 204.

52. *Index on Censorship*, February 1986, pp. 28–30.

53. Iraqi Solidarity Voice, March 1989, from *Wales Echo*, December 21, 1988.

54. One exception was the killing by thallium poisoning in January 1988 of Abdullah Rahim Sharif Ali, an Iraqi who ran a printing house in London. See chap. 4.

55. *Observer* (London), November 20, 1988.

CHAPTER 3: THE CONSTITUTION, THE JUDICIARY, AND FUNDAMENTAL RIGHTS

1. The translation of the Constitution used in this report is from Majid Kadduri, *Socialist Iraq* (Washington, D.C.: The Middle East Institute, 1978), pp. 183–98. A new constitution is said to be under preparation but had not been made public by the end of 1989.

2. Article 38(c).

3. Article 65(b).

4. Article 52. It is not specified what happens if the Assembly does not act within fifteen days.

5. Compare Article 42 with Article 52.

6. Article 52.

7. Article 54.

8. Article 55(b).

9. International Covenant on Civil and Political Rights, Human Rights Committee, Consideration of Reports Submitted by States Parties Under Article 40 of the Covenant, Second periodic reports of states parties due in 1985, Iraq, April 21, 1986, CCPR/C/37/Add 3, July 18, 1986, p. 46.

10. Amnesty International, "The Death Penalty in Iraq: Legal Aspects," May 21, 1987, p. 18.

11. Amnesty International, "The Death Penalty in Iraq: Legal Aspects," p. 19.

12. Amnesty International, "The Death Penalty in Iraq: Legal Aspects," pp. 19–20.

13. CCPR/C/37/Add.3, July 18, 1986, p. 27.

14. The claim that the provisions of the Covenant can be invoked in Iraqi courts was made by Iraqi officials to representatives of Amnesty International and in an Iraqi government report to the Human Rights Committee. See Amnesty International, "Summary of Report and Recommendations of an Amnesty International Mission to the Government of the Republic of Iraq," January 22–28, 1983, p. 6; and CCPR/C/37/Add.3, p. 3. So far as could be learned, Iraqi authorities have never cited a case in which a citizen exercised the right to invoke the provisions of the Covenant before a court in Iraq.

15. CCPR/C/37/Add.3, July 18, 1986, p. 27.

16. Article 20(c) of the Iraqi Constitution reads: "All trials shall be open to the public unless declared in camera."

17. U.S. Department of State, *Country Reports on Human Rights Practices for 1988*, Iraq (Washington, D.C.: Government Printing Office, 1988), pp. 1357–58. Persons accused of criminal acts are nonetheless subject to torture during interrogation and brutal treatment thereafter. See chap. 4.

18. Amnesty International, "The Death Penalty in Iraq: Legal Aspects," pp. 18–20.

19. CCPR/C/SR.203, March 26, 1980, para. 31.

20. For eyewitness testimony on this point, see chap. 4.

21. Middle East Watch interview with Hussein Shami, September 15, 1989.

22. See chap. 4; also Al-Khalil, *Republic of Fear*, p. 107.

23. Reported, among other places, in "Eight Thousand Civilian Kurds Have Disappeared in Iraq. What Has Happened to Them?" *A Report by the Preparatory Committee* (London, November 1987), p. 9.

24. Amnesty International, "Iraq, Children Innocent Victims of Political Repression," February 1989.

25. Retroactive punishment is also prohibited by the ICCPR, which in Article 15(1) specifies that "no one shall be held guilty of any criminal offense on account of any act or omission which did not constitute a criminal offense . . . at the time when it was committed."

26. RCC Resolution no. 461, March 31, 1980, cited in Amnesty International, "The Death Penalty in Iraq," p. 10.

27. Amnesty International, "The Death Penalty in Iraq," p. 17.

28. Article 3 of the Universal Declaration of Human Rights states: "Everyone has the right to life, liberty and security of person."

29. CCPR/C/37/Add.3, pp. 28–30.

30. For more on these death-penalty provisions, see chap. 2.

31. Law no. 141 of 1979, cited in Amnesty International, "The Death Penalty in Iraq," p. 10.

32. Amnesty International, "The Death Penalty in Iraq," pp. 15–16.

33. CCPR/C/37/Add.3, p. 27.

34. RCC Resolution no. 120 of January 29, 1986, cited in Amnesty International, "The Death Penalty in Iraq," p. 15.

35. See chap. 2.

36. Baath Party Eighth Regional Conference Report, 1974, cited in *Article 19, World Report: Information, Freedom and Censorship* (New York: Times Books, 1988), p. 256.

37. Various lists have been circulated of Communist and other left-wing journalists and writers arrested in 1979 and 1980 and not heard from since. *Article 19*, "Freedom of Information and Expression in Iraq," 1987, p. 24, names Dr. Hussain Qassim al-Aziz and Mohammad Karim Fathlah, both of *Al-Fikr Al-Jadid*; Suhair al-Jazzani, journalist and novelist; Abdul Salam al-Nasiri, director of *Al-Thaqafa Al-Jadida*; Dema Rashid, journalist; Fadil Al-Rubai, journalist and short-story writer; and Dana Tawfiq, former editor of the Kurdish newspaper *Alk Ta'aki*.

38. Law no. 70 of 1980, cited in *Article 19*, "Freedom of Information and Expression in Iraq," 1987, p. 28.

39. Raad Mushatat (pseudonym), in *Index on Censorship*, February 1986, p. 29.

40. Ali Hassan, in *Index on Censorship*, March 1981, "Profile—Modhaffar Al-Nawab."

41. See chap. 4.

42. *As Safir*, December 5, 1985, as cited in *Article 19*, "Freedom of Information and Expression in Iraq," p. 28.

43. John Kifner, "Once Proud Hosts, Iraqis Sour on Their Guest Correspondents," *The New York Times*, October 16, 1980.

44. *New York Times*, September 18, 1988.

45. Middle East Watch interview with Amy Kaslow, currently of *Christian Science Monitor*. Kaslow, at the time a freelance journalist, handled the videocamera problem by smearing toothpaste over the lenses, a measure she was obliged to repeat daily since each morning the cleaning personnel removed paste applied the previous evening.

46. For more on the organized practice of informing and on the secret-police agencies, see chap. 2.

47. For the text of this decree, see chap. 2.

48. CCPR/C/37/Add.3, pp. 40–41.

49. *U.S. News and World Report*, September 25, 1989, p. 40.

50. U.S. Department of State, *Country Reports on Human Rights Practices for 1988*, Iraq, p. 1361.

51. For more on this, see chap. 4.

52. For example, some 1,500 Kurds who returned to Iraq from Turkey in late 1988 after having fled poison-gas attacks in August and September of that year reportedly have not been heard from since. In addition, Dr. S. al-Hakim, director of the Organization of Human Rights in Iraq, filed a complaint with the U.N Human Rights Commission's Working Group on Disappearances about the disappearance of 33 Assyrian families who had returned under an offer of amnesty. See chap. 4.

53. See chap. 4.

54. Dawisha, "The Politics of War," in Axelgard, ed., *Iraq in Transition*, pp. 29–30.

55. See also "Genocide: Mass Deportation," a report published in London in 1989 by the Patriotic Union of Kurdistan, which lists fifteen ancient churches and monasteries destroyed or confiscated by the Iraqi government in the Kurdish region, the ancestral home of the Assyrians.

56. For more on this, see chap. 4.

57. Minority Rights Group Report No. 76, "The Jews of Africa and Asia" (London, 1987), p. 7.

58. Middle East Watch interview with Amy Kaslow, *Christian Science Monitor*.

59. Ibid.

60. Law no. 105 of 1970, as amended by law number 141 of 1979, set out the penalties for adherence to the Bahai faith. See Amnesty International, "The Death Penalty in Iraq," p. 10.

61. The means by which the Baath party's monopoly is assured are discussed in chap. 2.

62. The International Covenant on Economic, Social, and Cultural Rights guarantees, in Article 9, the "right of everyone to form trade unions and join the trade union of his choice."

63. Isam al-Khafaji, "Iraq's Seventh Year," *Middle East Report* (March–April 1988), pp.38–39.

64. U.S. Department of State, *Country Reports on Human Rights Practices for 1988*, Iraq, p. 1364.

65. U.S. Department of State, *Country Reports on Human Rights Practices for 1987*, Iraq, p. 1174; *Country Reports on Human Rights Practices for 1988*, Iraq, p. 1364.

66. International Labor Organization, *Report of the Committee of Experts, Observations Concerning Ratified Conventions*, 1989, pp. 281–282.

67. *Country Reports on Human Rights Practices for 1988*, Iraq, p. 1364.

68. Committee Against Repression and for Democratic Rights in Iraq, "Iraq: Terror and Executions," March 1981, p. 24.

69. "Egyptian Laborers Are Fleeing Iraq," *New York Times*, November 15, 1989.

70. Ibid.

CHAPTER 4: THE FORMS OF REPRESSION

1. These are procedures described by the Iraqi government in its report to the Human Rights Committee submitted under Article 40 of the International Covenant on Civil and Political Rights on April 21, 1986, CCPR/C/37/Add.3, pp. 33–35.

2. See chap. 3.

3. See, notably, U.S. Department of State, *Country Reports on Human Rights Practices for 1988*, Iraq, p. 1357.

4. The lower figure was given to Middle East Watch by a senior official of the State Department, the higher one by human rights groups, including the Organization of Human Rights in Iraq and the Committee Against Repression and for Democratic Rule in Iraq. The Federation Internationale des Droits de L'Homme, in its report of February 1986, "La Situation des Droits de l'Homme en Iraq," lists sixty-three Iraqi prisons in which political prisoners are reportedly held.

5. This account of Robert Spurling's detention and torture is based on an interview conducted by Middle East Watch with a U.S. diplomatic officer who dealt with the case, and on Spurling's testimony as reported by Amnesty International, "Torture in Iraq 1982–1984."

6. The Iraqi authorities' failure to notify the U.S. Interests Section in Baghdad of Spurling's arrest was a clear violation of Article 36 of the Vienna Convention on Consular Relations of April 24, 1963, to which both Iraq and the United States are parties.

7. Amnesty International, "Torture in Iraq 1982–1984," p. 10.

8. Amnesty International, "Torture in Iraq 1982–1984," p. 9.

9. For both meetings, Spurling was taken from prison to the Foreign Ministry, where Iraqi officials remained in attendance. U.S. officials were never allowed to visit him in prison.

10. Amnesty International, "Torture in Iraq 1982–1984," pp. 20–21.

11. *The Sun* (London), September 8, 1981.

12. *The Sun* (London), September 8, 1981, p. 8.

13. *The Sun* (London), September 8, 1981, pp. 18–19.

14. Amnesty International, "Torture and Executions in Iraq: Summary of Amnesty International's Concerns," March 1986, p. 5.

15. Article 22(a) of Iraq's constitution reads: "The dignity of Man is guaranteed. Any kind of physical or psychological torture shall be prohibited."

16. UNGA resolution 3452, December 9, 1975.

17. These arguments are set out in Iraq's report of April 1986 to the Human Rights Committee, CCPR/C/37/Add.3, p. 32.

18. Ibid., p. 32.

19. Article 7 of the International Covenant on Civil and Political Rights states: "No one shall be subjected to torture or to cruel, inhuman or degrading treatment or punishment." Article 4 of the Covenant stipulates that no derogation is permitted from Article 7 even for reason of public emergency.

20. Nabil al-Janabi, "Memoir of Terror," *Index on Censorship*, January 1989. Al-Janabi repeated his account in an interview with Middle East Watch.

21. Ibid.

22. "Medical Report on Mr. Nabil Jamil Al-Janabi," Medical Foundation for the Care of Victims of Torture; examining physician Tom Landau MRCS LRCP.

23. Reprinted by permission of *Index on Censorship*.

24. Amnesty International, "Iraq: Evidence of Torture," April 29, 1981, p. 5.

25. Ibid., p. 6.

26. Amnesty International, "Torture in Iraq 1982–1984," pp. 10–11.

27. Ibid., p. 11.

28. Amnesty International, "Iraq—Children Innocent Victims of Political Repression," February 1989, Section 6.

29. Ibid.

30. Ibid.

31. Ibid.

32. *Official Journal of the European Communities*, No. C125/132, May 11, 1987, resolution dated April 9, 1987.

33. Since they were first issued, for the year 1979, until the latest volume, for 1988, the State Department's *Country Reports on Human Rights Practices* have stated that torture is frequently or routinely practiced in Iraq's prisons.

34. *Middle East Contemporary Survey, 1977–78* (Boulder, Colorado: Westview Press, for Tel Aviv University), p. 519.

35. Al-Khalil, *Republic of Fear*, p. 52.

36. Dana Adams Schmidt, *New York Times*, January 27, 1969.

37. See Marr, *The Modern History of Iraq*, p. 214, and Al-Khalil, *Republic of Fear*, pp. 53–54.

38. Marr, *The Modern History of Iraq*, p. 217. See also Al-Khalil, *Republic of Fear*, pp. 6–7.

39. Marr, *The Modern History of Iraq*, p. 230.

40. *Middle East Contemporary Survey, 1979–80*, p. 505.

41. See *Amnesty International Report 1983*, Iraq; and Organization of Human Rights in Iraq, London, "Execution of Two Iraqi Doctors," November 24, 1988.

42. Milton Viorst, "The View from the Mustansiriyah," *The New Yorker*, October 12, 1987.

43. *Observer* (London), October 16, 1988, "Death Purge by Saddam."

44. *Amnesty International Bulletin*, March 6, 1989.

45. The Baath regime had two objectives in joining with the Communists, and both were related to its dispute with the Kurds over their demands for autonomy. The regime sought to win the Iraqi Communists away from the Kurds, whom the Communists had backed and on whose side they had frequently fought, and to win from the Soviet Union the arms needed to put down the Kurdish rebellion. Both objectives were attained.

46. For example, *Iraq Solidarity Voice* (London), a publication of the Committee Against Repression and for Democratic Rule in Iraq, reported in its July 20, 1988,

issue the execution in early 1987 of Rasmiya Jabr al-Wazni, a teacher and member of the Iraqi Women's League and the Iraqi Communist party, who was arrested in Baghdad in 1985.

47. *Amnesty International Bulletin*, November 14, 1979.

48. *Middle East Contemporary Survey, 1979–80*, p. 515.

49. Federation Internationale des Droits de l'Homme, "La Situation des Droits de l'Homme en Iraq," February 1986 (Middle East Watch translation). The Iraqi government acknowledged the execution of the six members of the al-Hakim family several weeks later but claimed that they had been duly charged and tried for espionage and subversion.

50. Ibid. Dr. S. al-Hakim, director of the Organization of Human Rights in Iraq, confirmed in an interview with Middle East Watch the accuracy of this account.

51. See chap. 2.

52. *Middle East Contemporary Survey, 1980–81*, p. 585, from *Foreign Report*, July 23, 1981.

53. Marr, *The Modern History of Iraq*, p. 308.

54. *Amnesty International Report 1978*, Iraq.

55. *Amnesty International Report 1979*, Iraq.

56. *Amnesty International Report 1981*, Iraq.

57. *Amnesty International Report 1982*, Iraq.

58. *Amnesty International Report 1983*, Iraq.

59. *Minority Rights Group #2* report, Iraq. Ubaidullah Barzani had been associated with the Baghdad regime since 1974 and was considered a turncoat by the Barzani family.

60. Ibid.

61. "Baghdad-Kurd Talks on Autonomy Collapse," *Washington Post*, July 29, 1984.

62. *Amnesty International Report 1986*, Iraq.

63. Amnesty International Urgent Action Bulletin, "Iraq: Extrajudicial Executions," December 20, 1985.

64. Amnesty International, "The Death Penalty in Iraq: List of Persons Reported Executed/Sentenced to Death Between January 1985 and January 1987," May 21, 1987.

65. Amnesty International, "Iraq: Executions," March 1988.

66. "Reign of Terror Sweeps Iraq's Scientific Community," *New Scientist* (London), April 2, 1981.

67. Ibid.

68. *Amnesty International Report 1988*, Iraq.

69. Ibid.

70. Al Sharq Al Awsat in Arabic, January 14, 1988, Foreign Broadcast Information Service: Near East and Far Asia (FBIS-NES-88-010), January 17, 1988.

71. *The Times* (London), January 23, 1988.

72. *Amnesty International Report 1983*, Iraq.

73. Amnesty International, "Torture and Executions in Iraq," March 1986.

74. Amnesty International Newsletter, September 1982.

75. Ibid.

76. *New Scientist* (London), April 2, 1981.

77. Amnesty International Newsletter, September 1982.

78. The word *pardon* was typed in capital letters in the ambassador's letter.

79. It should be noted that 1979 and 1980 were years when substantial numbers of disappearances began to be reported in Iraq.

80. According to an unconfirmed report, after returning to Baghdad in 1980 Ambassador al-Jabiri was fired from the Foreign Ministry and interrogated for several months on suspicion of working for a foreign power. He is said today to be living in Baghdad and working as a teacher.

81. This account is based on an interview conducted by Middle East Watch with a former official who served as advisor to a governmental delegation to the United Nations Human Rights Commission's session of 1980 and who had direct knowledge of the case.

82. Report of the Working Group on Enforced or Involuntary Disappearances, Iraq, E/CN.4/1989/18 (January 18, 1989).

83. "Eight Thousand Civilian Kurds Have Disappeared in Iraq, What Has Happened to Them?" Report by a Preparatory Committee (established by the Kurdish Democratic Party), London, November 1987, pp. 14–15.

84. Report of the Working Group on Enforced or Involuntary Disappearances, Iraq, E/CN.4/1989/19 (January 18, 1989).

85. Ibid.

86. Middle East Watch interview with Dr. S. al-Hakim, director of the Organization of Human Rights in Iraq, who filed the case on behalf of the Assyrian National Congress.

87. Ibid.

88. Al-Khalil, *Republic of Fear*, Marr, *The Modern History of Iraq*, and Sluglett, *Iraq Since 1958*, all discuss the deportations of the late 1970s and early 1980s. There is no agreed figure for the number of those deported.

89. Al-Khalil, *Republic of Fear*, p. 19.

90. At a meeting of the United Nations Commission on Human Rights held in Geneva on February 27, 1987, Iraq's representative stated that "no Iraqi citizens had been deported to Iran. What had happened was that [my] Government had expelled to Iran some hundreds of Iranians—foreigners—that had been living in Iraq" (E/CN.4/1987/SR.36, March 3, 1987).

91. Al-Khalil, *Republic of Fear*, pp. 19 and 135–37; *World Refugee Survey: 1985*, pp. 61–62; and Helms, *Iraq*, pp. 145–46.

92. See Helms, *Iraq*, pp. 145–46.

93. Ibid., p. 31n37.

94. *World Refugee Survey: 1985*, p. 61, puts the number of those expelled to Iran in the late 1970s and early 1980s at one hundred thousand, and adds: "Reports indicate that many Iraqi citizens, because of their suspect Iranian ancestry, have been stripped

of their citizenship and possessions and sent on foot through the Zagros Mountains to the Iranian border."

95. "The Tragedy of the Iraqi Deportees," a brochure published in 1986 by the Commission for the Welfare of Iraqi Refugees, a Shia exile group based in London, puts the number of Shia businessmen expelled in this first round-up at five hundred. Others interviewed by Middle East Watch cited a figure of between one and two hundred.

96. *New Scientist* (London), April 2, 1981, p. 4.

97. In negotiations with Iraq following the cease-fire of August 1988, Iran placed their number at two hundred thousand.

98. Article 4 of the Fourth Geneva Convention of August 12, 1949, states, inter alia: "Persons protected by the Convention are those who, at a given moment and in any manner whatsoever, find themselves, in case of a conflict or occupation, in the hands of a Party to the conflict or Occupying Power of which they are not nationals."

99. Paper transmitted UNHCR headquarters to Middle East Watch's consultant on October 13, 1989, by UNHCR office, Washington, D.C., in reply to written inquiry of September 20, 1989.

100. Middle East Watch interview with Abdul Wahab al-Hakim.

101. Al-Khalil, *Republic of Fear*, p. 136.

102. For example, Iraq's new ambassador to the United States, formerly ambassador in London, Dr. Mohammed Sadiq al-Mashat, is understood to be of a family of Iranian origin.

CHAPTER 5: THE KURDISH MINORITY

1. The Soviet Union also has a Kurdish population, dispersed among the southern Soviet Republics. The USSR's census of 1970 showed a total Kurdish population of 278,463. See Gerard Chaliand, ed., *People without a Country* (London: Zed Press, 1982), p. 222.

2. Anthony Hyman, "Elusive Kurdistan" (London: Center for Security and Conflict Studies, n.d.), p. 8; Helsinki Watch, *Destroying Ethnic Identity: The Kurds of Turkey*, March 1988.

3. Article 5(b).

4. Official Iraqi government translation, reprinted in Minority Rights Group, "The Kurds," 1975, pp. 22–23.

5. Chaliand, *People without a Country*, pp. 170 and 176–78. Also see Minority Rights Group, "The Kurds," pp. 22–23.

6. See chap. 4.

7. Chaliand, , pp. 171–72.

8. Edmund Ghareeb, *The Kurdish Question in Iraq* (Syracuse, N.Y.: Syracuse University Press, 1981), pp. 28–29. The Kurds were not of one mind, however, on this or

other issues; Mosul and Arbil voted to approve Faisal's appointment. (See Minority Rights Group, "The Kurds," p. 18.)

9. Chaliand, *People without a Country*, pp. 159–60.

10. Cited in ibid., p. 161, from League of Nations Special Report on Progress in Iraq.

11. Cited in ibid., p. 162, from League of Nations, "Report by the Commission set up by the 30 September 1924 resolution to investigate the question of the frontier between Turkey and Iraq."

12. Ibid., p. 163.

13. Ibid., p. 178.

14. Ibid., p. 179.

15. *Middle East Contemporary Survey, 1977–78*, p. 521.

16. *Amnesty International Report 1977*, p. 299.

17. Ibid.

18. Ibid.

19. *Amnesty International Report 1978*, p. 258.

20. *Middle East Contemporary Survey, 1978–79*, p. 569.

21. *Middle East Contemporary Survey, 1981–82*, p. 597.

22. The other leading group was the Kurdish Democratic Party, now under the leadership of Masoud Barzani, Mulla Mustapha's son.

23. *Al Thawra*, March 10, 1983, as cited in *Middle East Contemporary Survey, 1982–83*, p. 574.

24. *Middle East Contemporary Survey, 1982–83*, p. 575.

25. *Al Thawra*, August 29, 1986, as cited in *Middle East Contemporary Survey, 1986–87*, p. 382.

26. *Al Thawra*, June 17, 1986, cited in *Middle East Contemporary Survey, 1986–87*, p. 382.

27. For details of abuses in Kurdish areas of Iraq, see chap. 4.

28. See chap. 4.

29. "Chemical Weapons Use in Kurdistan: Iraq's Final Offensive," *A Staff Report to the Senate Committee on Foreign Relations*, by Peter W. Galbraith and Christopher Van Hollen, Jr. (Washington, D.C.: Government Printing Office, September 21, 1988) p. 18. Galbraith and Van Hollen visited Turkey between September 11 and 17, 1988.

30. Ibid., p. 14.

31. Marie Colvin, "Kurds Flee Chemical Terror into Turkey," *Sunday Times* (London), September 11, 1988.

32. Galbraith and Van Hollen, "Chemical Weapons Use in Kurdistan," p. 15.

33. Unpublished letter from Gwynne Roberts to Tom McCarthy, U.N. Human Rights Centre, Geneva, June 1, 1989.

34. Ibid.

35. Ibid.

36. *International Herald Tribune*, September 5, 1988.

37. Excerpts published in "Refugees, A Barometer of Genocide," Bill Frelick, *World Refugee Survey*.

38. Middle East Watch interview with U.S. officials. The U.S. embassy in Ankara reported that Turkish villages along the Iraqi border had been affected by gas that blew over from the Iraqi army's attacks on August 25–27.

39. Clyde Haberman, *New York Times*, September 11, 1988.

40. Clyde Haberman, *New York Times*, September 12, 1988.

41. Gary Thatcher, *Christian Science Monitor*, September 15, 1988.

42. This agreement was made public in a statement made by the Iraqi ambassador in Turkey and reported by *The Economist*, June 18, 1983.

43. Clyde Haberman, in "Turkey Reports Kurdish Refugees Showed No Signs of Iraqi Gassing," *New York Times*, September 10, 1988, reported: "Journalists who visited the border region found that the refugees' stories were often confusing and lacking in detail."

44. Milton Viorst, "Poison Gas and Genocide: The Shaky Case Against Iraq," *Washington Post*, October 5, 1988. Viorst spoke only of gas attacks "on rebel positions," implying that whatever use was made of gas was against legitimate military targets. Viorst ignored testimony that the main target of Iraqi gas attacks was Kurdish civilians in villages.

45. Galbraith and Van Hollen, "Chemical Weapons Use in Kurdistan," Summary of Key Findings.

46. "Winds of Death: Iraq's Use of Poison Gas Against its Kurdish Population," Report of a Medical Mission to Turkish Kurdistan by Physicians for Human Rights, February 1989, p. 1.

47. Middle East Watch interview with Gwynne Roberts, September 19, 1989, and "Winds of Death," a television film produced by Roberts and Wykeham Films Limited. Also see Reuters, "Laboratory Finds Poison Gas Traces in Iraqi Soil Samples," November 22, 1988, and "Poison Gas Traces are Found in Iraq," *New York Times*, December 4, 1988.

48. "Turkey Opposes an Inquiry into Poison Gas Issue," *New York Times*, September 15, 1988.

49. Patrick E. Tyler, "Iraq Denies Using Chemical Gas Against the Kurds," *Washington Post*, September 16, 1988.

50. "Kurds are No-Shows in Iraqi Press Event," *International Herald Tribune*, September 19, 1988.

51. Ibid.

52. *New York Times*, September 18, 1988.

53. Seth Carus, "The Genie Unleashed: Iraq's Chemical and Biological Weapons Production," *The Washington Institute Policy Papers* (Washington, D.C., 1989), p. 3.

54. "Iraq Denies Chemical Warfare, Scores U.S.," *Washington Times*, March 7, 1984.

55. In meeting between Congressmen Mel Levine and Robert Torricelli and Foreign Minister Tariq Aziz in Baghdad, January 1988.

56. Carus, "The Genie Unleashed," p. 7.

57. Ibid., p. 1.

58. Ibid., p. 38.

59. Ibid., pp. 29–35.

60. The Reuter Library Report, September 15, 1988, "Arab U.N. Envoys Voice Concern Over Gas Charges Against Iraq," and *Jane's Defense Weekly*, December 24, 1988. When criticized for this statement, Ambassador Maksoud complained that his intent had been distorted; all he had meant to say was that all chemical weapons should be banned (cf. press conference 10/14/88, LEXIS NEXIS).

61. Middle East Watch interview with Professor Theodor Meron of New York University School of Law.

62. According to one expert consulted for this study, the Iraqi government may have made small-scale use of poison gas against the Kurds as early as the Kurdish rebellion of 1974–75. Middle East Watch interview with U.S. official.

63. "The Kurdish Program," Cultural Survival, New York, bulletin dated June 15, 1988.

64. U.N. Security Council document S/19823 (French), April 25, 1988, p. 16 (Middle East Watch translation).

65. Ibid. and S/19823 Add.1, May 10, 1988. The Iraqi soldiers may have been victims of Iranian poison-gas attacks, or they could have been the inadvertent victims of their own army's use of chemical weapons.

66. "Les Kurdes sous le Gaz," *Le Monde*, July 21, 1988.

67. Middle East Watch interview. The ICRC was so shocked by the gassings at Halabja that it set aside its customary reserve and issued a press statement: "Chemical weapons have been used, killing a great number of civilians in the province of Suleimanieh. . . . The use of chemical weapons, whether against military personnel or civilians, is absolutely forbidden by international law and is to be condemned at all times" (ICRC press release number 1567, March 23, 1988).

68. Edward Mortimer, writing in *The Financial Times* (London), March 16, 1989, said 6,350 people were killed in the chemical-weapons attack at Halabja on March 1988.

69. Patrick E. Tyler, *Washington Post*, September 16, 1988.

70. The U.S. State Department's human rights report on Iraq for 1988 states that "approximately half a million Kurdish and Assyrian villagers" have been relocated. See *Country Reports on Human Rights Practices for 1988*, p. 1355.

71. Statement by Saddam Hussein, Reuters, and Iraqi News Agency, July 21, 1978, cited in *Middle East Contemporary Survey, 1977–78*, p. 521.

72. *Middle East Contemporary Survey, 1978–79*, p. 569.

73. Ibid., p. 569.

74. *The Independent* (London), June 3, 1989. Ambassador al-Mahat was appointed to Washington in September 1989.

75. A senior Iraqi official in Arbil, quoted by Associated Press and reported in *The Times* (London), June 6, 1989.

76. The Iraqi government's claim that the depopulated security zone has been extended beyond the Kurdish areas, to the south of Iraq, has not been verified by any independent source. The city of Basra, which lies no more than ten kilometers from

the Iranian border, and the port of Fao, hardly more than a kilometer from Iran across the Shatt al-Arab waterway, are being rebuilt. Both were much more heavily shelled during the war with Iran than any city or town in Kurdish areas of Iraq.

77. At the current official rate of exchange maintained by the Iraqi government, one Iraqi dinar is valued at U.S.$3.14. On the black market, one U.S. dollar is said to bring approximately 3.5 Iraqi dinars.

78. Iraqi Embassy Press Office, Washington, D.C.

79. Middle East Watch interview with Ambassador al-Anbari, June 27, 1989. In August 1989 Ambassador al-Anbari transferred to New York to become Iraq's Permanent Representative to the United Nations.

80. "War in the Persian Gulf: The United States Takes Sides," a staff report to the Committee on Foreign Relations, United States Senate, October 9, 1987, p. 16.

81. Ibid.

82. "Kurds Can't Go Home Again, Because Their Homes are Gone," *New York Times*, September 18, 1988.

83. "Scorched Kurdish Villages Bear Witness to Iraqi Assault," *Washington Post*, September 17, 1988.

84. See notably, Patrick E. Tyler, "Iraq Targets Kurds for Relocation," *Washington Post*, April 30, 1989.

85. *The Times* (London), April 24 and June 12, 1989. Mullah Muhammad is believed to have been released from detention in August 1989.

86. The drama of the forced evacuation of Qalat Diza was followed closely by the British press. See, among others, articles in *The Sunday Times*, April 9, 1989; *The Guardian*, April 14, 1989; and *The Times*, June 12 and 14, 1989.

87. Yves Heller, "L'ordre règne au Kurdistan irakien," *Le Monde*, September 21, 1989.

88. Statement by Dr. Abdul Amir al-Anbari, Iraqi ambassador to the United States, June 1989.

89. Middle East Watch interview with State Department officials. These officials do not rule out the possibility that some of the difference between the State Department figure and that of Kurdish opposition groups could stem from a difference in counting methods, such as a group of villages being counted as a single unit rather than as several individual units.

90. David McDowall, in talk entitled "Developments in Kurdish Nationalism Today," given at the Royal Institute of International Affairs, London, September 12, 1989.

91. Yves Heller, *Le Monde*, September 21, 1989 (Middle East Watch translation).

92. Tim Kelsey, "Resettled Kurds Mourn Lost Mountains," *The Independent* (London), August 19, 1989.

93. *Revised and Updated Report on the Question of the Prevention and Punishment of the Crime of Genocide*, prepared by Mr. B. Whitaker, United Nations Economic and Social Council, E/CN.4 Sub.2/1985/6, July 2, 1985, p. 5.

94. "Chemical Weapons Use in Kurdistan—Iraq's Final Offensive," a staff report

to the Senate Committee on Foreign Relations, September 21, 1988, p. 4: "Where Iraq's policy consitutes genocide, within the meaning of the Genocide Convention, may be debated if the standard used for genocide is that of the elimination of an entire race. However, we find no question that Iraq's policy in Kurdistan has the characteristics of genocide."

95. Asked at the time about Kurdish charges that the Mardin camp victims had been poisoned by Iraq, a U.S. government official commented to Middle East Watch that the Kurds were "undermining their credibility by making such wild accusations."

96. The following account is based on a Middle East Watch interview with Gwynne Roberts on September 18, 1989, and on an unpublished article by Roberts.

97. See chap. 4.

98. Unpublished article by Gwynne Roberts.

99. Unpublished article by Gwynne Roberts.

CHAPTER 6: THE TREATMENT OF IRANIAN PRISONERS OF WAR

1. Press conference by Iraqi Foreign Minister Tariq Aziz, New York, December 14, 1989, Foreign Broadcast Information Service (FBIS-NES-89-240), December 15, 1989.

2. See "Prisoners of War in Iran and Iraq," *The Report of the Mission Dispatched by the Secretary General, January 1985*, United Nations Security Council document S/16962, pp. 30–33.

3. Ibid., p. 32.

4. Ibid., p. 35.

5. See *Report of the Mission Dispatched by the Secretary General on the Situation of Prisoners of War in the Islamic Republic of Iran and Iraq*, United Nations Security Council document S/20147, August 24, 1988.

6. Ibid., p. 32.

7. Ibid., pp. 24–25.

8. Ibid., pp. 25–26.

9. Ibid., p. 29.

10. Ibid., p. 30.

11. See Alan Cowell, "For Prisoners of War, Boys' Summer Camp?" *New York Times*, February 17, 1988.

12. Press conference by Ian Brown, Terre des Hommes Director of the Ramadi 7 camp school, August 23, 1989, in Paris. Terre des Hommes bulletin.

CHAPTER 7: THE UNITED STATES AND IRAQ

1. Middle East Watch interview with unnamed U.S. State Department official, June 1989.

2. Interests sections are offices maintained in one another's capitals by states that have broken diplomatic relations. The offices are operated under the umbrella of a protecting power. Belgium played this role for the United States and India for Iraq. Interest sections can be headed by midlevel diplomats or by diplomatic officers of senior rank who act as ambassadors in all but name. The U.S. Interests Section in Baghdad entered the latter category in 1977, and full diplomatic relations were restored in 1984 when an ambassador from the United States was appointed.

3. Fuad Mattar, *Saddam Hussein: The Man, the Cause and the Future* (London: Third World Press, 1981), p. 108.

4. The Hussein quote is from "U.S. Department of State Background Notes," Iraq, October 1987, p. 6, which mentions only that the Iraqi president's remark was made "to a visiting U.S. Congressman."

5. Middle East Watch interviews with U.S. Department of Agriculture officials.

6. Iraq continued, however, to harbor the PLO terrorist group headed by Abu Abbas which carried out the *Achille Lauro* hijacking in 1985 in which U.S. citizen Leon Klinghofer was killed (Middle East Watch interview with U.S. official).

7. "U.S. Eyes Sanctions Against Iraq," *Christian Science Monitor*, August 31, 1988.

8. David Ottaway, *Washington Post*, October 6, 1988.

9. "Iraq deals embarrass U.S.," *The Guardian* (London), May 4, 1989.

10. "Citing Atom Link, U.S. Halts Pumps Bound for Iraq," *International Herald Tribune*, May 6–7, 1989.

11. Agriculture Department officials consulted on this point denied knowledge of any weighing of human rights considerations prior to approval of the credits. One State Department source claimed that the matter had "been looked at" but further remarks suggested that whatever consideration had been given was of a wholly informal and cursory nature. The Export-Import Bank is not required to consider human rights issues in deciding whether to extend loans.

12. Section 502B of the Foreign Assistance Act.

13. David Ottaway, *Washington Post*, October 6, 1988. State Department officials also advanced this argument in discussing the issue with Middle East Watch. It offers a convenient excuse, for without having U.S. observers in the combat zone there is almost no way that use of the helicopters in combat could be verified.

14. Ibid.

15. By contrast, on August 29, 1989, the State Department recalled Ambassador Sol Polansky from Sofia in protest of Bulgaria's mistreatment of its ethnic Turkish minority.

16. Testimony before the Subcommittee on Europe and the Middle East of the House Foreign Affairs Committee.

17. Address delivered at the annual dinner of Middle East Institute, Washington, D.C.

18. *Congressional Record*, September 26, 1988, H.8345.

19. "U.S. Eyes Sanctions Against Iraq," *Christian Science Monitor*, August 31, 1989.

20. The *New York Times*, January 12, 1989, carried the full text of the declaration.

21. See chap. 5.

22. Jonathan Randal, *Washington Post*, January 7, 1989.

23. Ibid.

24. The resolution was submitted by Australia, Belgium, Canada, Denmark, West Germany, Luxembourg, the Netherlands, Norway, Portugal, Sweden, and the United Kingdom. Greece, Ireland, Italy, and Spain later joined as sponsors. Of the sponsors, Belgium, Canada, West Germany, Portugal, Sweden, the United Kingdom, Italy, and Spain were actual members of the Human Rights Commission. The other sponsors acted in their observer capacity. Commission rules permit observers to sponsor resolutions but not to vote on them.

25. This is a procedure created by Economic and Social Council resolution 1503 under which individuals and nongovernmental organizations may submit complaints against U.N. member states for consistent patterns of gross violations of human rights. If deemed admissible by the Subcommission on Discrimination and the Protection of Minorities, these complaints are forwarded to the Human Rights Commission for examination in closed session. The commission may, however, as it did in the case of Iraq, reject the subcommission's recommendation.

CHAPTER 8: COVERING UP HUMAN RIGHTS VIOLATIONS

1. *Middle East Economic Digest*, February 17, 1989, reports that seven Iraqi police officers, including an officer of the rank of colonel, were to be put on trial for the murder and torture of three Iraqi citizens falsely accused of killing a Baath party official in the city of Najaf. This is the first such reported prosecution, but the outcome of the trial and the sentences given the accused, if any, have not been announced. In the absence of more detailed information, the significance of this isolated case is unclear.

2. See chap. 4.

3. See chap. 5.

4. The first acknowledgment came from Foreign Minister Tariq Aziz, during a visit to Bonn on July 1, 1988, a little more than four years after the United Nations and the United States first announced that they had reliable information that Iraq was using poison gas against Iran.

5. As noted in the introduction to this book, in August 1989 an Iraqi official issued an oral invitation to members of the Subcommission on Prevention of Discrimination and Protection of Minorities to visit Iraq to look into allegations of use of chemical weapons against Iraq's Kurdish minority and to study Iraq's program of forced relocation of its Kurdish population. It appears that this invitation was no more genuine than others issued periodically by Iraqi envoys, as described later in this chapter. According to U.S. government sources, at the time the original report went to press, Iraq had not responded to efforts to arrange a visit on terms that would permit a valid inquiry.

6. U.N. Economic and Social Council, Commission on Human Rights, Forty-fifth session, *Report of the Working Group on Enforced or Involuntary Disappearances*, E/CN.4/1989/18, January 18, 1989, p. 47.

7. David Pallister, "Kurd Appeals to Thatcher for Help," *The Guardian* (London), May 31, 1989.

8. "Consideration of Reports Submitted by States Parties Under Article 40 of the Covenant," second periodic report of states parties due in 1985, Addendum, Iraq, CCPR/C/37/Add.3, July 18, 1986, p. 5. Iraq's report was submitted on April 21, 1986, a little more than six months after the reported arrest of some 300 Kurdish children aged ten to fourteen, held hostage for opposition activities of their parents. Some of these children were believed to have been tortured to death in captivity. See Amnesty International, "Torture and Executions in Iraq," March 1986. In a letter to the editor of *The New York Times* dated July 7, 1986, Iraq's ambassador to the United States, Nizar Hamdoon, denied Amnesty's report.

9. See chap. 3.

10. See chap. 5.

11. See chap. 4.

12. MP Ann Clwyd, Letter to the Editor, *The Independent* (London), April 7, 1989.

13. Ambassador al-Mashat was transferred to a new appointment as Iraqi ambassador to the United States. He arrived in Washington to take up his new post on September 6, 1989. His predecessor, Dr. Abdul Amir al-Anbari, moved to New York to become ambassador to the United Nations.

14. See chap. 5.

15. State Department Press Briefing, June 15, 1988. By "those countries," the State Department's spokesperson meant states of the Middle East that have Kurdish minorities.

16. *Index on Censorship*, September 1988, pp. 45–46.

17. Middle East Watch interview with delegate to the U.N. Human Rights Commission's session of February–March 1989. The procedure of resolution 1503, as noted, offers an avenue for individuals and nongovernmental organizations to present complaints against governments that engage in a consistent pattern of gross violations of human rights.

18. It was in the course of debate over this resolution that the Iraqi observer delegate issued the oral invitation to subcommission members to visit Iraq to look into allegations of chemical-weapons use against unarmed civilians and of human rights abuses in Iraq's forced-resettlement program (see the introduction). As indicated earlier, the invitation appears to have been nothing more than a tactical maneuver designed to win the votes needed to block the resolution.

19. Iraqi officials say their government plans to spend some $35 billion on development projects over the next few years. See *Christian Science Monitor*, August 31, 1989.

20. The Senate amendment nonetheless survived and became law in November 1989.

21. "United States–Iraq Business Forum Bulletin," August 1989. The bulletin states that the delegation was led by the forum's chairman, A. Robert Abboud, chairman and CEO of First City Bancorporation of Texas, and that former senator Charles H. Percy and Alan Stoga of Kissinger Associates accompanied it. It lists the following companies as having participated in the visit: Amoco Corp., Baker Hughes Inc., Bankers Trust Co., Bell Helicopter Textron Inc., Caltex Petroleum Corp., Caterpillar Inc., General Motors Corp., Hunt Oil Co., M. W. Kellog Co., Mobil Oil Corp., Occidental International Exploration and Production Co., Westinghouse Electric Corp. and Xerox. The bulletin also reported that on May 1, 1989, representatives of General Motors Corp. signed an agreement with Hussein Kamel Hassan, minister of industry and military industrialization (also reputedly head of the Presidential Special Security Agency) for the manufacture of 90,000 Oldsmobiles in Iraq.

22. Letter from Nizar Hamdoon, ambassador of Iraq, to Edward J. Van Kloberg, III, August 22, 1985. Document filed by Edward Van Kloberg and Associates with the Foreign Agents Registration Unit, U.S. Department of Justice.

23. Van Kloberg and Associates Disclosure Statement, December 28, 1987, filed with Foreign Agents Registration Unit, U.S. Department of Justice. In response to Middle East Watch's inquiry, Warren Nelson, a senior member of Congressman Aspin's staff for the House Armed Services Committee, denied that either Van Kloberg and Associates or the Iraqi government had been involved in any way in the August 27 op-ed piece.

24. Justice Department Registration Statement filed by Paul, Hastings, Janofsky and Walker, May 22, 1986.

25. Disclosure statements filed by Paul, Hastings, Janofsky and Walker with the Justice Department. In addition, the Iraqi government paid the firm another $146,172 for legal services, the precise nature of which was not disclosed.

26. Middle East Watch was told that the Iraqi government has from time to time attempted to improve its image in the British media by trying, unsuccessfully, to suborn certain British journalists.

27. Letter from Dominic Morris, private secretary to Prime Minister Thatcher, to Dr. S. al-Hakim, director, Organization of Human Rights in Iraq, August 2, 1989. On this subject, Morris added that "Sir Geoffrey Howe made our concerns clear to the Iraqi Ambassador on 19 July as did Mr. Waldegrave when he met the Iraqi Deputy Foreign Minister on 12 July."

28. David McDowall, "Developments in Kurdish Nationalism Today," a talk given at Chatham House, September 11, 1989.

29. October 12 and 19, 1987.

30. Luis Matias Lopez, *El Pais*, September 25, 1989.

31. Middle East Watch interview with Amy Kaslow, at the time of her sojourn in Baghdad a freelance journalist, now a correspondent for the *Christian Science Monitor*. Kaslow, as noted, dealt with the problem of the videocameras by smearing toothpaste over their lenses.

32. Brookings Institution, 1984.

33. Center for International and Strategic Studies, 1988.

34. Robert G. Neumann, in Frederick W. Axelgard, ed., *Iraq in Transition*, pp. ix and x. This book, published in 1986 and designed, in the words of its editor, to foster "an expanding understanding of the country," offered chapters on war and oil, the politics of war, economic outlook, Iraq in the Gulf, and Iraq and the superpowers, but no discussion whatsoever of Iraq's human rights violations.

35. Frederick W. Axelgard, "Iraq: The Postwar Political Setting," *American-Arab Affairs* (Spring 1989).

36. This, it should be pointed out, will not be a new development. Article 26 of the Interim Constitution of 1970 states: "The constitution shall guarantee freedom of opinion, publication, meeting, demonstration, forming of political parties, unions and societies."

37. Axelgard, "Iraq."

38. Ian Black, "Strong Saddam Presence at Poll," *The Guardian* (London), April 3, 1989.

39. *Le Monde*, September 21, 1989 (Middle East Watch translation).

40. Baghdad INA in Arabic, 0640 GMT, November 28, 1988, FBIS-NES-88-230, November 30, 1988. President Hussein was speaking before the Arab Lawyers Union, a pan-Arab group of lawyers and jurists affiliated with the Baath party and headquartered in Baghdad.

BIBLIOGRAPHY

Al-Khalil, Samir. *Republic of Fear*. Berkeley and Los Angeles: Univ. of California Press, 1989.

Abdulghani, J. M. *Iran & Iraq: The Years of Crisis*. London: Croom Helm, 1984.

Ismael, Tareq Y. *Iran and Iraq: Roots of Conflict*. 1st ed. Syracuse, N.Y.: Syracuse Univ. Press, 1982.

Axelgard, Frederick. "A New Iraq?" *The Washington Papers*. Washington, D.C.: Center for Strategic and International Studies, 1988.

Axelgard, Frederick, ed. *Iraq in Transition*. Boulder, Colo.: Westview Press, 1986.

Ayubi, Shaheen, and Tahir-Kheli, Shirin, eds. *The Iran-Iraq War: New Weapons, Old Conflicts*. New York: Praeger, 1983.

Baram, Amazia. "Qawmiyya and Wataniyya in Ba'thi Iraq." *Middle Eastern Studies* 19 (April 1983): 188–200.

Batatu, Hanna. "Class Analysis and Iraqi Society." *Arab Studies Quarterly*, vol. 1, no. 3 (1979): 229–44.

———. "Iraq's Underground Shi'a Movements: Characteristics, Causes, and Prospects." *Middle East Journal*, vol. 35, no. 4 (1981): 178–94.

———. *The Egyptian, Syrian, and Iraqi Revolutions: Some Observations on Their Underlying Causes and Social Character*. Washington, D.C.: Georgetown Univ. Press, 1984.

———. *The Old Social Classes and the Revolutionary Movements of Iraq*. Princeton, N.J.: Princeton Univ. Press, 1978.

Committee Against Repression and for Democracy in Iraq. *Saddam's Iraq*. London: Zed Books. 1989.

Chaliand, Gerard. *People Without a Country*. London: Zed Press, 1982.

Cooley, John K. "Conflict With the Iraqi Left." *Jerusalem Quarterly* 9 (1978): 131–44.

Dann, Uriel. *Iraq Under Qassem: A Political History, 1958–1963*. New York: Praeger, 1969.

Finkelstein, J. J. *The Ox That Gored*. Philadelphia: American Philosophical Society, 1981.

Gabbay, Rony E. *Communism and Agrarian Reform in Iraq*. London: Croom Helm, 1978.

Ghareeb, Edmund. *The Kurdish Question in Iraq*. Syracuse, N.Y.: Syracuse Univ. Press, 1981.

Helms, Christine Moss. *Iraq: Eastern Flank of the Arab World*. Washington, D.C.: The Brookings Institution, 1984.

Ingrams, Doreen. *The Awakened: Women in Iraq*. London: Third World Centre, 1983.

Jawad, Sa'ad. *Iraq and the Kurdish Question 1958–70*. London: Ithaca Press, 1981.

Kadduri, Majid. *Socialist Iraq*. Washington, D.C.: The Middle East Institute, 1978.

Kedourie, Elie. "Continuity and Change in Modern Iraqi History." *Asian Affairs*, vol. 62, no. 2 (1975): 140–46.

Kelidas, Abbas, ed. *The Integration of Modern Iraq*. London: Croom Helm, 1979.

King, Ralph. *The Iran-Iraq War: The Political Implications*. London: International Institute for Strategic Studies, 1987.

Marr, Phebe. *The Modern History of Iraq*. Boulder, Colo.: Westview Press, 1985.

Mattar Faud. *Saddam Hussein: The Man, The Cause and the Future*. London: Third World Press, 1981.

Niblock, Tim, ed. *Iraq, The Contemporary State*. London: Croom Helm, 1979.

Our Tyrannized Cities: Statistical Survey of Aggressions of Baathist Regime of Iraq Against Iranian Cities and Residential Areas. Tehran: War Information Headquarters, Supreme Defense Council, 1983.

Petran, Tabitha. "Social Structures and Class Formation in Iraq." *Monthly Review*, vol. 32, no. 7 (1980): 46–53.

Price, David Lynn. "Baghdad: Return to the West?" *Washington Quarterly* 2 (Autumn 1979): 143–46.

Rubin, Barry. *The Politics of Terrorism*. Washington, D.C.: Foreign Policy Institute, School of Advanced International Studies, The John Hopkins University, 1989.

Shikarah, Ahmed Abd al-Razzaq. *Iraqi Politics 1921–41: The Interaction Between Domestic Politics and Foreign Policy*. London: Laam Ltd., 1987.

Simon, Reeva S. *Iraq Between the Two World Wars: The Creation and Implementation of a Nationalist Ideology*. New York: Columbia Univ. Press, 1986.

Sluglett, Marion and Peter. *Iraq Since 1958*. London: Kegan Paul International, 1987.

Strok, Joe. "Oil and the Penetration of Capitalism in Iraq: An Interpretation." *Peuples Mediterraneens—Mediterranean Peoples* 9 (1979): 125–52.

Tarbush, Modhammed A. *The Role of the Military in Politics: A Case Study of Iraq to 1941*. London and Boston: Kegan Paul International, 1982.

Turner, Arthur Campbell. "Iraqi Pragmatic Radicalism in the Fertile Crescent." *Current History*, vol. 81, no. 471 (1982): 14–17.

The 1968 Revolution in Iraq: Experience and Prospects: The Political Report of the Eighth Congress of the Arab Ba'th Socialist Party in Iraq. January 1974. London: Ithaca Press, 1979.

HUMAN RIGHTS OR HUMANITARIAN ORGANIZATIONS: PUBLICATIONS

Article 19 (London)

Amnesty International (London)

Commission for the Welfare of Iraqi Refugees (London)
Committee Against Repression and for Democratic Rights in Iraq (London)
Federation Internationale des Droits de l'Homme (Paris)
Institut Kurde (Paris)
International League for Human Rights (New York)
Minority Rights Group (London)
Organization of Human Rights Group (London)
Parliamentary Human Rights Group (London)
Physicians for Human Rights (Boston)
The Kurdish Program, Cultural Survival (New York)
U.S. Committee for Refugees (Washington)

PERIODICAL PUBLICATIONS

Index on Censorship
Kurdish Times
Middle East Report
Middle East Economic Digest
Middle East International
Newsweek
The Economist
The Middle East Times
US News and World Report
United Nations. Annual Reports of the United Nations Human Rights Commission
    Working Group on Enforced or Involuntary Disappearances
United Nations. International Labor Organization Reports.
United Nations. Reports of the United Nations Rights Commission—Special
    Rapporteur on Summary of Arbitrary Execution.
United Nations. Reports of the United Nations Human Rights Commission—Special
    Rapporteur on Torture.
United Nations. Periodic Reports of the Government of Iraq to the United Nations
    Human Rights Committee (International Covenant on Civil and Political Rights).
United Nations Security Council, Reports of Missions Dispatched by the Secretary
    General to Investigate Allegations of the Use of Chemical Weapons in the Conflict
    between the Islamic Republic of Iran and Iraq.
U.S. Department of State Country Reports on Human Rights Practices, 1979 to
    Present.
U.S. Senate. Staff Reports to the Committee on Foreign Relations. *War in the
    Persian Gulf: The U.S. Takes Sides.* November 1987.
U.S. Senate. Staff Reports to the Committee on Foreign Relations. *Chemical
    Weapons Use in Kurdistan: Iraq's Final Offensive.* October 1988.

MAJOR DAILY PRESS AND OTHER

The Christian Science Montior (U.S.)
The International Herald Tribune (Paris)
The New York Times (U.S.)
The Washington Post (U.S.)
The Independent (U.K.)
The Financial Times (U.K.)
The Guardian (U.K.)
The Times (U.K)
Le Monde (France)
El Pais (Spain)
Baghdad Observer (Iraq)
Al Thawra (Iraq)
Foreign Broadcast Information Service (U.S. Government)

Index

Abu Abbas, Mohammed (PLO official), 108, 151n
Abu Nidal, 18, 104
Aflaq, Michel (founder of Baath party), 9, 135n
Amir, Abd al-Anbari (ambassador to United States), x, 87
Amn (State Internal Security), 17
Amn al-Khass (Special Security), 18
Amnesty International: mission to Baghdad (1983), x, 117, 120; on retroactive punishment, 27; on Baath Party, 28; on arrests and torture, 42–43, 46; on thallium poisonings, 57–58
Arbil, Kurdish Autonomous Region, 55, 56, 83–90 passim
Arif, Abd al-Rahman (president of Iraq, 1966–68), 4, 14
Arif, Abd al-Salaam (president of Iraq, 1963–66), 3, 4
Assyrian minority, 33, 35, 39, 58, 63, 86, 106, 107
Aziz, Tariq (Iraqi foreign minister), 78, 82, 109–110, 152n

Baath Socialist Party, ix, xiii, 3, 4, 8–13, 28, 31, 120, 128; policy of "terror and reward," ix, 133n; founding of, 9; membership of, 9–10; and Regional Command, 10, 22, 135n; control of press, 30; on emigration, 32; and persecution of Jews, 35, 49; purge of, 39, 50, 51; and political killings, 49; and Kurds, 70–96 passim; and General Intelligence Directorate, 122; and Communists, 144n

Baghdad: in Iran-Iraq war, 5, 6, 134n; and Jewish community, 33, 35–36, 49; and Egyptian workers, 37–38; Baghdad University, 45, 47, 119; morgue, 47; execution of mayor, 51; and Shia community, 52; and thallium poisoning, 58; and U.S. embassy, 110
Baghdad Pact, 3, 101
Bahai faith, 28, 36, 140n
Bakr, Ahmad Hassan al- (president of Iraq, 1968–79), 4, 8, 14, 49, 51
Barzani, Mulla Mustapha (Kurdish leader), 2, 4, 54, 61, 70, 71, 73, 87
Barzinji, Sheikh Mahmoud (Kurdish leader), 71
Basra, 37, 49, 148n

Central Intelligence Agency (CIA), 71
Christian minority, xiii, 1, 3, 4, 35, 39, 49, 63, 86
Code of Criminal Procedure, 40
Committee Against Repression and for Democratic Rule in Iraq, 141n
Commodity Credit Corporation (CCC), 103, 107, 108, 111, 131

Death penalty: and Baath Party, 12–13, 32; and cult of personality, 16, 130; and judiciary, 24; and Covenant, 27; in Iraqi Penal Code, 27–28, 133n
Dehok, xii, 86, 91

Edward J. Van Kloberg and Associates, 123
Egypt, 63, 89, 101, 103; and Egyptian